Inconvenient and Uncomfortable
© Copyright 2018 Marshall Wordsworth

ALL RIGHTS RESERVED. No part of this book may be reproduced or transmitted in any form or by any means, electronic or mechanical including photocopying, scanning, recording, or by any other information storage and retrieval system without the express written permission of the author.

ISBN-10: 1724576763
ISBN-13: 9781724576767

INCONVENIENT AND UNCOMFORTABLE

TRANSCENDING JAPAN'S COMFORT WOMEN PARADIGM

Marshall Wordsworth

I dedicate this work to the women laborers, the *ianfu* and their equivalents, who gave courage, strength, and comfort to the soldiers who fought and paid the ultimate sacrifice for their beloved countries.

Contents

Prologue	9
Introduction: Comfort Women - Japan's Military Brothel System	17
Part I: Systematic Forcible Abduction/Recruitment/Conscription	
A. Complexity in the Battleground: The Philippines	23
B. Illegal Forcible Roundup: Semarang Case in the Dutch East Indies	39
C. Japan's Annexed Territory: The Korean Peninsula	49
D. The Paradigmatic Story of Systematic Forcible Recruitment by the Japanese Military	67
Part II: Sexual Slavery	
A. Terminology and Types of Comfort Stations	85
B. Purpose of Implementing a Comfort Women System	90
C. Comfort Station in Hankow, China	94
D. Details from a Comfort Station Manager's Diary	101
E. Comfort Station as a Business Enterprise	110
F. Former Comfort Woman Mun Ok-chu	116
G. Human Drama and Intimacy at Comfort Stations	124
Part III: The Numbers Question: Origin of the 200,000 Claim	
A. Kakō Senda	137
B. Conflation with Teishintai/Chongsindae	139
C. First Comfort Station in Shanghai, China	144
D. Estimates Based on Military Records	146
Part IV: Putting Things in Perspective for the 21st Century	
A. Other Military Brothels Since World War II	157
B. Japan's Past Compensations, Reparations, and Apologies	162
C. The 2015 Accord with South Korea	167
D. Transcending the Comfort Women Paradigm	170

Prologue

Since the early 1990s, Japan has been accused of atrocious war crimes and gross violations of human rights for its implementation and use of the comfort women system throughout the Pacific War.[1] The comfort women (called *ianfu* in Japanese), defined by the Western media as women and girls who were abducted, forcibly recruited, conscripted, or forced into 'sexual slavery' at military brothels for the Japanese Imperial Forces during and before World War II[2], have become a highly emotional issue that has not only caused diplomatic tensions, in particular between Japan and South Korea, but has also resulted in bitter clashes within Asian communities in North America, West Europe, and Australia in recent years. In these conflicts outside Japan, the Japanese groups have expressed their opposition to the erecting of comfort women statues and monuments that purport to commemorate the comfort women who suffered during Japan's territorial invasion and occupation in parts of Asia until the end of World War II. Whereas the proponents

---

1 Also referred to as the Asia Pacific War and Japan's Fifteen-Year War by some scholars, the period from Japan's invasion of Manchuria in 1931 to its surrender in August 1945 to end World War II. Soh, C. Sarah, *The Comfort Women: Sexual Violence and Postcolonial Memory in Korea and Japan*, The University of Chicago Press, Chicago, (2008), xii, xvii.

2 One of the earliest newspaper articles on comfort women in English is "Japan's wartime army prostitutes", *Korea Times*, Monthly English Edition, Los Angeles, CA, Jan. 20, 1992:6. It reads, "Historians estimate that as many as 200,000 young Korean women between the ages of 16 and 20 were forcibly taken from their homes in poor, rural areas to work as sex slaves in Manchuria, China and, later, throughout Southeast Asia."

of these memorials advocated greater awareness of inherent issues regarding women's rights and the ongoing abuses by human trafficking, the Japanese counterparts maintained that the issue of Imperial Japan's comfort women has nothing to do with the nations where the memorials are being considered in addition to taking exception to its prevailing narrative in the West.

In September of 2017, the city of San Francisco erected statues portraying comfort women of Chinese, Filipino, and Korean ancestry in St. Mary's Square, making it the first major city in America to do so. Osaka, Japan's third largest city, announced its intention to revoke the 60-year long sister-city relationship with San Francisco out of protest in November of that year.[3]

Other U.S. cities such as Glendale, CA, and Palisades Park, NJ, have erected either a comfort woman statue or monument in the past several years. In fact, the city of Brookhaven, GA, and Fort Lee, NJ joined other cities even after Japan and South Korea had entered into a bilateral accord on December 28, 2015 to resolve the comfort women issue "finally and irreversibly."[4]

Such strong language by Japan and South Korea calls for a serious and impartial analysis of diplomatic circumstances, as well as of the controversial aspects of the comfort women issue. The prevailing narrative that has been recited by the

---

3 Taylor, A. (Nov. 25, 2017) Osaka mayor to end sister city status with San Francisco over 'comfort women' statue. *The Washington Post.* (https://www.washingtonpost.com/news/worldviews/wp/2017/11/25/osaka-mayor-to-end-sister-city-status-with-san-francisco-over-comfort-women-statue/?utm_term=.c45ca276f0ee)

4 Announcement by Foreign Ministers of Japan and the Republic of Korea at the Joint Press Occasion, Dec. 28, 2015. (http://www.mofa.go.jp/a_o/na/kr/page4e_000365.html)

proponents of the comfort women redress movement can be broken into three elements: the Japanese military engaged in a) an institutionalized, systematic abduction[5], forcible recruitment or conscription; b) of up to or more than 200,000 women[6]; c) for 'sexual slavery' as a response to the sexual needs of its soldiers.

While certain original source documents that proponents of the redress movement reference to validate their claim have been available for some time, other documents unearthed in recent years would make any objective reader more inquisitive and inclined to seek further information on the realities of Japan's comfort women system. This study will also introduce and analyze lessor known works on comfort women, including publications that have yet to be translated into English. Moreover, a new and more comprehensive interpretation of some documents already available to the English-speaking audience will be presented, and it is up to

---

5 As examples, inscriptions at the Palisades Park Public Library, NJ, and the Veterans Memorial, Eisenhower Park, Westbury, NY include, respectively, "In memory of the more than 200,000 women and girls who were abducted by the armed forces of the government of Imperial Japan," and "In remembrance of more than 200,000 women and girls who were abducted for the use of sexual slavery by the armed forces of the government of Imperial Japan."

6 In recent years, the 200,000 figure has been replaced with 'hundreds of thousands' after China became a major proponent of the comfort women issue, and the language utilized by the San Francisco activists reflects this change. Prior to China's relatively recent participation in the debate, 200,000 had been universally accepted and recited by the redress movement activists, with the assertion that most of the women having been Korean.

the reader to contemplate whether a different viewpoint from the prevailing narrative has merit.

But before each of these elements are examined in detail by reviewing various documents and records, some of which were discovered in recent years for the first time, the descriptions of the comfort women who arrived in Rabaul (then territory of Australia) in January of 1942 by a civilian POW serve as a rather interesting prelude.

Gordon Thomas, editor of *The Rabaul Times*, surrendered to the Japanese forces on January 23, 1942, and within weeks was assigned to operate a commercial freezer and ice plant – the Supply Headquarters of the Japanese army around Rabaul, New Britain (present-day Papua New Guinea). His taking care of the food supply such as meat, fish, and vegetables along with ice in the freezer allowed him to interact not only with the Japanese soldiers but also with the comfort women during a period of three years and seven months, and a book based on his diary during that time was published in 2012.

Below is his impression of the comfort women when they first arrived in Rabaul:

> ... one day I found myself again on wharf work. This time the vessel had brought a cargo of Korean females, resplendent in their various-coloured kimonos, fancy hair-styles and clip-clopping wooden shoes (or 'geta' as they are called in Japan).[7]
>
> There were over 200 'Ladies of Thousand Delights'; gay, chattering little bodies, laughing and running

---

[7] Thomas, Gordon, *Prisoners in Rabaul: Civilians in Captivity 1942-1945*, Australian Military History Publications, Loftus, (2012), p.29.

about like children- ... Our task consisted of carrying their bundles and suitcases from the deck of the vessel to load on lorries waiting near the wharf.[8]

His colleague, a well-known priest in the area who assisted in handling the luggage jokingly remarked, "I wonder what His Holiness would say if he knew I was portaging for prostitutes?"[9]

After briefly commenting on the arrival of Japanese women in Rabaul as well, here are additional observations regarding the comfort women by Thomas:

> Three weeks after the landing of the Japanese troops there were over 3,000 of these little ladies working at top pressure, to satisfy the requirements of some 100,000 thousand troops.[10]

> Each man was entitled to a permit to visit once every two weeks.[11]

> To my mind, the prostitutes were the outstanding reason why the local Asiatic women were not molested by the invaders.[12]

---

8 Ibid., p.30.
9 Ibid.
10 Ibid.
11 Ibid.
12 Ibid., p.31.

He even wrote about women belonging to two brothels having a physical confrontation before the *Kempeitai* (Japanese military police) came to restore order:

> ... I heard cries and a general rush of army and navy personnel towards No 94. A dozen of the Korean ladies were having a full-scale brawl, with the beauties of No. 96 having it out with the lassies of No 94. Each was shouting and, presumably cursing, at the top of her voice and every now and then making a grab at an adversary, tearing and pulling at hair and flimsy garments.[13]

Thomas then notes his observation of the changing environment in Rabaul:

> During the second quarter of 1943, Allied planes scarcely gave us a day's rest.[14]

According to a notebook he kept, depopulation of civilians in Rabaul began around December of 1943 as a result of the continuous aerial assaults by the Allies, but the comfort women's safety appears to have been given priority:

> Many of the Ladies of Pleasure had already departed during the previous month and December saw the last of them amid a flourish of cheers and waving as they sped through the streets, seated on top of their beds and baggage. They were the one remaining splash of

---

13 Ibid., p.99.

14 Ibid., p.106.

colour in a town of dark drab grey and green landscape and uniformed humanity.[15]

Unfortunately, the fate that awaited the women was nothing short of tragic:

> However, they were doomed, these 'Little Ladies of Ten Thousand Delights' for, after having catered untiringly to the desires of the servicemen for nearly two years and collected a sum sufficient to pay off the mortgage on the old Korean homestead, their ships were bombed a day or so out of Rabaul and only half-a-dozen or so escaped to tell the tale. It was a sad ending for those Little Ladies, who had gone through so much and I always admired their cheerfulness.[16]

Although Japanese cargo ships continued to leave Rabaul until the end of February of 1944, almost all of the airplanes had been annihilated or withdrawn by then.[17] Japan's occupation of Rabaul was quickly coming to an end, foreshadowing its eventual defeat in the Pacific.

These comments by a civilian Australian are unique in that even though he was a member of Japan's wartime enemy, he did not partake in any actual combat, and by being given an important role to be in charge of the food supply

---

15 Ibid., p.112.

16 Ibid.

17 The United States Strategic Bombing Survey (Pacific) The Allied Campaign against Rabaul, Naval Analysis Division, Washington, 1946, p.24. (https://babel.hathitrust.org/cgi/pt?id=wu.89051200715;view=1up;seq=5)

on an island the Japanese forces occupied for several years, his opinions of the comfort women can be invaluable and perhaps as objective as those of any third party. Thomas' book will be revisited as numerous aspects of the comfort women system are carefully scrutinized.

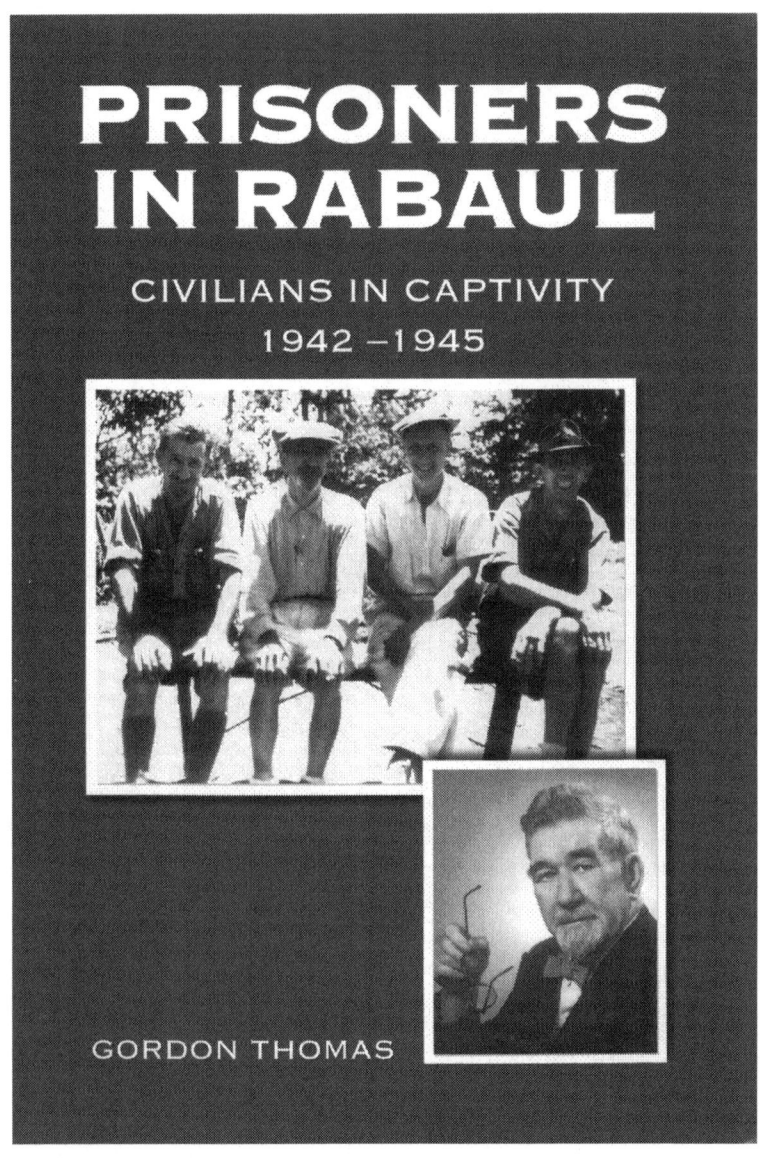

Introduction:
Comfort Women - Japan's Military Brothel System

As mentioned in the Prologue, the comfort women redress movement spearheaded by Korean nationalists and transnational human rights activists has been promoting the narrative of Japanese Imperial Forces as having engaged in a) an organized, systematic abduction, forcible recruitment or conscription; b) of up to or more than 200,000 women; c) for sexual slavery. In short, the allegation involves an institutionalized sexual enslavement by the Imperial Japanese military through some form of coercion, and the element of the 'institutionalized, systematic' means carried out to procure the women will be explored first. Accounts by former comfort women on the recruiting process will be the main focus to establish the extent of its coercive, forcible nature.

Next, in Part II, the element of sexual slavery will be examined, with careful review given to recorded information by individuals having performed various functions at comfort stations in addition to the accounts by former comfort women. Together with the recruiting process, the environment in which the women labored will provide a working foundation to engage in an attempt to analyze the comfort women system in a more comprehensive manner. The last element of the prevailing narrative, the 200,000 women (or more recently, 'hundreds of thousands')[1] claim will be discussed in Part III, from its very origin and how it became part of the continuous 'paradigmatic story' of the comfort women issue for over two decades.

Finally, Part IV will cover post-World War II military brothels during conflicts in Asia, Japan's apologies and financial commitments since its unconditional surrender in August 1945, and an unconventional stance on comfort women will be taken to conclude this study.

---

[1] The placard found near the comfort women statues in San Francisco reads: "This monument bears witness to the suffering of hundreds of thousands of women and girls, euphemistically called "Comfort Women", who were sexually enslaved by the Japanese Imperial Armed Forces in thirteen Asia-Pacific countries from 1931 to 1945."

PART I

Systematic Forcible
Abduction/Recruitment/Conscription

A. Complexity in the Battleground: The Philippines

Of the three comfort women statues in San Francisco, one depicts a Filipino woman. Maria Rosa Henson continues to be the most famous as her 1996 autobiography describes her ordeal as a captured victim of rape and violence. While her account involves abduction by Japanese soldiers, her book confirms the fact that she had been a member of Hukbalahap, an anti-Japanese communist guerrilla group prior to being taken away to a garrison.[1] In fact, her abduction took place while she was "carrying food and medicine to help the Filipino guerrilla movement," in this case the Hukbalahap, in April 1943.[2]

The Japanese military began to invade the Philippines in December of 1941, and battles with the native Filipinos continued long after the U.S.-Philippine forces surrendered in May 1942. In other words, resistance to the Japanese occupation continued to persist until General Douglas MacArthur returned three years later, and the Philippine islands remained a battleground that only recently had become Japan's occupied enemy territory. As such, the circumstances surrounding Maria Henson and others identified as Filipino comfort women involved ongoing hostilities, with the threat of loss of life at any given time, both to the Filipino natives as well as the Japanese soldiers. With opposition forces such as Hukbalahap present, the Japanese military probably

---

1 Henson, Maria Rosa, *Comfort Woman: A Filipina's Story of Prostitution and Slavery under the Japanese Military*, Rowman & Littlefield Publishers Inc., Maryland, (1999), xv.

2 Soh, p.131.

considered many of the Filipino population as unfriendly, if not downright antagonistic. The estimates of guerrilla organizations at their peak exceeded 100 that consisted of about 270,000 activists and associates.[3]

Moreover, the Japanese military only managed to control 30 percent of the Philippine islands during its occupation, and thus, "wonton" means of addressing the needs of its soldiers seem to have taken place[4], at the very least in certain instances. Since the majority of identified Filipino sexual victims such as Maria Henson were residents of Luzon and Pinay, two islands known for popular guerrilla activities, it can be argued that the Japanese troops tended to regard any civilian, especially from those islands, "as a possible guerrilla collaborator" and women were probably spared their lives but instead suffered by reason of "belonging to the enemy."[5]

Even so, the issue of comfort women in the Philippines becomes more complicated as the U.S. military forces in the Pacific Theater kept records of what they have accumulated as part of their intelligence gathering. The Allied Translator and Interpreter Section (ATIS) Supreme Commander for the Allied Powers Research Report dated November 15, 1945 includes a section entitled "Amenities in the Japanese Armed Forces" that dealt with information available to ATIS up to March 31, 1945.

Under the section "Brothels," contents of a bound printed booklet titled "Rules for Authorized Restaurants and Houses of Prostitution in Manila" issued by Lt. Col. Ōnishi, Manila

---

3 Henson, xv.

4 Ibid.

5 Ibid.

District Line of Command Squad in February 1943 include regulations of all sorts including Business Operation, Management, Hygiene, Discipline, and so on. Examples of them are as follows:

Part One - General Regulations

1. In these regulations, authorized restaurants will be taken to mean those places designated by the Officer in Charge of MANILA Sector Line of Communications Duties, with the sanction of the army commanding general, as eating places for soldiers and army civilian employees. House of relaxation should be taken to mean those places designated by the Officer in Charge of MANILA Sector Line of Communications Duties, with the sanction of the army commanding general, which maintain hostesses, geisha, or waitresses for the entertainment of soldiers and army civilian employees.[6]

Part Two - Business Operation

5. Persons planning to operate authorized restaurants or houses of relaxation must submit the following documents to the officer in charge of MANILA Sector Line of Communications Duties. Managers must be Japanese who have had some business experience.

a. Application for permission to open business: three copies [Appendix A, Form No.1].

---

6 Allied Translator and Interpreter Section (ATIS) Supreme Commander for the Allied Powers Research Report, Amenities in the Japanese Armed Forces, Nov. 15, 1945, No. 120 (hereinafter "ATIS Research Report No. 120"), p.9, I.G. No. 6310 B.I.D. No. 1228 Restricted.

b. Statement of business plans: three copies [Appendix A, Form No.2].
c. Affidavit: three copies [Appendix A, Form No.3].
d. Personal History: three copies.

6. Persons receiving permission to open business will thereupon determine the number of personnel needed, and will submit three copies of their business personnel list [Appendix A, Form 4, one copy of the personal histories of employees and three copies of requests for authorization of the hostesses (geisha and waitresses – Appendix A, Form No. 5). When preparations are complete, the Officer in Charge of MANILA Sector Line of Communications Duties, will be informed, and business may commence after the inspection of the establishment and the physical examination of the employees.[7]

10. Hostesses (geisha, waitresses[8], maids) may, as a general rule, be re-hired at the expiration of their term of contract. (This does not apply in persons who have not been overseas at least a year. Those wishing to continue their employment will so notify the Officer in charge of MANILA Sector Line of Communications Duties for his approval. When the medical authorities consider it suitable to discontinue the services of anyone for reasons of health, they will so inform the Officer in Charge of MANILA Sector

---

7 Ibid.

8 A generic term such as waitress (*shakufu* in Japanese) was sometimes used to refer to comfort women. Soh, p.69.

Line of Communications Duties. The latter will facilitate the return home of such persons.

11. Managers of houses of relaxation will make arrangements for the following:
   a. Bedding in all bedrooms.
   b. Cuspidors in all bedrooms and waiting rooms.
   c. Sterilizers and medicines in lavatories and other designated places.
   d. Regulations and price charts in the waiting rooms.
   e. Hostesses' (geisha and waitresses) name-certificates in waiting rooms and individual rooms (Those of diseased hostesses will be marked in red.) Apart from the above, the establishment of entertainment and rest facilities for guests and the inauguration of other means of relaxation will be encouraged.[9]

Part Three - Management
   13. Management will present guests of the house of relaxation with a 'relaxation-ticket' in exchange for an army ticket, and will record all receipts of these 'relaxation-tickets' by the hostesses.[10]

   16. Half of the income of the hostesses will be allotted to the managers.[11]

---

9 ATIS Research Report No. 120, pp.9-10.

10 Ibid., p.10.

11 Ibid.

18. On the last day of each month, managers will submit a report on business conditions to the Officer in charge of Manila Sector Line of Communications Duties.[12]

21. As far as possible, managers will encourage the hostesses (geisha and waitresses) to save money.[13]

Part Four – Hygiene
23. Hostesses will ordinarily be examined by an army physician once a week at a designated place.[14]

25. Persons failing the physical examinations or receiving unfavorable diagnosis will be forbidden to entertain guests while under treatment.[15]

The final section of these regulations involves, among other matters, a policy that prohibits minors from working as a comfort woman:

Part Six – Regulations for Special Clubs
11. The Officer in Charge of MANILA Sector Line of Communications Duties, will, as a general rule, not permit the employment of minors as geisha or waitresses. In certain circumstances however, minors may be employed as maids.[16]

---

12 Ibid.

13 Ibid.

14 Ibid.

15 Ibid.

16 Ibid., p.12.

RESTRICTED

139

ALLIED TRANSLATOR AND INTERPRETER SECTION
SUPREME COMMANDER FOR THE ALLIED POWERS

RESEARCH REPORT

SUBJECT:	AMENITIES IN THE JAPANESE ARMED FORCES	I. G. No. 6310
		B.I.D. No. 1228
DATE OF ISSUE	15 November 1945	No. 120

SUMMARY:

1. This report covers information available at ATIS up to 31 March 1945 on amenities furnished by the Japanese to their armed forces.

2. There has been no attempt to establish the existence of rules regarding the availability for purchase or gratuitous issue of canteen stores, since there is a great variation, depending upon the type of troops and the area, in the handling of amenities.

3. Information has also been given as to the availability to the troops of such amusements as shows, movies, geisha entertainment, and brothels.

4. References are quoted regarding the amount of war news passed on to troops by field newspapers, bulletins, and radios.

HNB/SRE/CHR/rb
Distribution H

SIDNEY F. MASHBIR
COLONEL S.C
CO-ORDINATOR

SOURCES: Captured Documents.
Statements of Prisoners of War.

(INFORMATION SHOULD BE ASSESSED ACCORDINGLY)

RESTRICTED

BROTHELS

KOROR where they had places of amusements, shops, cinemas, and brothels: He occasionally went to ARAKABESAN:"
ATIS Interrogation Report, Serial No. 101, page 8

c. South West PACIFIC Area

'1) Prisoner of War YOSHIDA, Kazuo, Lance Corporal, member of 6 Field Artillery Regiment, captured TOROKINA Area, 23 March 1944, stated:
"During the summer of 1943, several Japanese actresses arrived at RABAUL to entertain Japanese troops. Heard that same troupe came to entertain air corps personnel and some officers at ERVENTA. Names of actresses in troupe known to prisoner of war: TAKAMINE, Miyeko; YANAKI, Sakko. After staying two to three days at ERVENTA, they returned to JAPAN because of American bombing."
(SOPAC Interrogation Report, Serial No. 01439, page 36)

'2) Prisoner of War KISHIMOTO, Hachiro, Superior Private, member of 23 Infantry Regiment, captured BOUGAINVILLE, 6 April 1944, stated:
"In CHINA, the so-called Entertainment War Relief Groups (probably similar to American United Service Organization organized by politicians, veterans of war, and other associations, were sent to various combat units. They usually brought Geisha girls with them and held stage shows. Famous actors, actresses, singers, and comedians visited soldiers to entertain but they had not come as far as BOUGAINVILLE."
(SOPAC Interrogation Report, Serial No. 01122, page 3)

9. BROTHELS

a. Regulations

1. *MANILA*

a. Bound printed booklet ' entitled "Rules for Authorized Restaurants and Houses of Prostitution in MANILA", issued February 1943 by Lieutenant Colonel ONISHI, MANILA District Line of Communication Squad.

Part One—General Regulations

"1. In these regulations, authorized restaurants will be taken to mean those places designated by the Officer in Charge of MANILA Sector Line of Communications Duties, with the sanction of the army commanding general, as eating places for soldiers and army civilian employees. Houses of relaxation should be taken to mean those places designated by the Officer in Charge of MANILA Sector Line of Communications Duties, with the sanction of the army commanding general, which maintain hostesses geisha or waitresses for the entertainment of soldiers and army civilian employees.

"2. Managers may close down or suspend the operation of their establishments only with the permission of the officer in charge of MANILA Sector Line of Communications Duties.

"3. If and when the various managers meet with difficulties, the officer in charge of MANILA Sector Line of Communications Duties may either close the business or temporarily suspend it. In such cases, the managers will present a statement for recompense for any losses or for

1. The translation of a police report listing medical inspection of brothels consisting of a group of loose sheets which accompanied this document, although not actually part of the original, is relevant to the contents and has been reproduced as Appendix B.

any other inconvenience.

"4. Authorized restaurants and houses of relaxation will be used only by soldiers and army civilian employees.

Part Two—Business Operation

"5. Persons planning to operate authorized restaurants or houses of relaxation must submit the following documents to the officer in charge of MANILA Sector Line of Communications Duties. Managers must be Japanese who have had some business experience.

"a. Application for permission to open business: three copies (Appendix A, Form No. 1).
"b. Statement of business plans: three copies Appendix A, Form No. 2).
"c. Affidavit: three copies (Appendix A, Form No. 3).
"d. Personal history: three copies.

"6. Persons receiving permission to open business will thereupon determine the number of personnel needed, and will submit three copies of their business personnel list (Appendix A, Form No. 4), one copy of the personal histories of employees and three copies of requests for authorization of the hostesses (geisha and waitresses, Appendix A, Form No. 5). When preparations are complete, the Officer in Charge of MANILA Sector Line of Communications Duties, will be informed, and business may commence after the inspection of the establishment and the physical examination of the employees.

"7. Managers intending to change the personnel of their establishments must secure the permission of the Officer in Charge of MANILA Sector Line of Communications Duties. Hostesses geisha and waitresses wishing to leave the establishments must submit a request therefore Appendix A, Form No. 6). When the hostesses (geisha and waitresses) and other employees are to be replaced, a request for permission to do so must be submitted (Appendix A, Form No. 7).

"8. Managers intending to increase the number of hostesses (geisha and waitresses), maids and others will so inform the Officer in Charge of MANILA Sector Line of Communications Duties. The date and time for the physical examinations by the medical authorities will be announced for each occasion. On completion of the physical examinations, the examination charts together with copies of personal histories or identification papers will be submitted to the Officer in Charge of MANILA Sector Line of Communications Duties. Permission is necessary before anyone joins the establishment.

"9. The location of and the buildings used as authorized restaurants and houses of relaxation must have the approval of the Officer in Charge of MANILA Sector Line of Communications Duties. In the future, managers who cannot maintain discipline may be removed. The Officer in Charge of MANILA Sector Line of Communications Duties will be informed of any repairs contemplated for army-controlled houses.

10 Hostesses (geisha, waitresses, maids) may, as a general rule, be re-hired at the expiration of their term of contract. (This does not apply to persons who have not been overseas at least a year. Those wishing to continue their employment will so notify the Officer in Charge of MANILA S for Line of Communications Duties for his approval. When the medical authorities consider it suitable to discontinue the services

Appendix A.—FORMS REQUIRED BY MANILA BROTHELS.

1. Form No. 1

   Application for permission to open business: army authorized restaurants or houses of relaxation.
   Home address:
   Present address:
   Name:
   Date of birth:
   I hereby present application to open an authorized restaurant (house of relaxation). I enclose a statement of business plans, an affidavit and my personal history.
   Date:
   Applicant's name and seal:
   To: Officer in Charge, MANILA Sector Line of Communications Duties.

2. Form No. 2

   Statement of business plans
   a. Capital: yen.
   b. Business partners: (yes or no)
   c. Number of rooms.
   d. Place of business.
   e. Names of hostesses (geisha and waitresses) (Indicate whether Japanese, Formosan or Filipino).
   f. Expected date of assembly of employees (geisha, maids, waitresses, other employees).
   Date:
   Name and seal:
   To: Officer in Charge, MANILA Sector Line of Communications Duties.

3. Form No. 3

   Affidavit
   I hereby promise, that on receipt of permission to open an authorized restaurant (house of relaxation), I will abide by all the rules and regulations, allow or cause no disturbances and agree to close or suspend business on order at the convenience of the army.
   Date:
   Name and seal of manager:
   To: Officer in Charge, MANILA Sector Line of Communications Duties.

4. Form No. 4

List of Employees						
Name	Date of Birth	Sex	Professional Name	Home Address	Advance Payments	Position
YAMASHITA, Kazuyasu						Manager
YAMAMOTO, Haruko						Waitress
YAMASHITA, Tatsu						Principal Hostess
ITATSU, Sueichi						Office Employee
NAGAHIDE, Hide						Bell-boy

   Date: Seals of above persons
   To: Officer in Charge, MANILA Sector Line of Communications Duties

APPENDIX A

5. Form No. 5

Request for authorization of hostesses (geisha and waitresses)
Home residence:
Name:
Date:
Professional name:
Date of arrival in PHILIPPINES:
I hereby request authorization for the above geisha (waitress). Enclosed please find copies of contract and agreement.
Date:
Name and seal of applicant:
Name and seal of manager:
To: Officer in Charge, MANILA Sector Line of Communications Duties.

---

6. Form No. 6.

Request for permission for hostesses (geisha and waitresses) to leave the establishments.
Home residence:
Present residence:
Name:
Date of birth:
Professional name:
I hereby submit this application for permission to leave the establishment, with the following information:
  (a) Reason:
  (b) Intended destination:
  (c) Amount of forced savings.
  (d) Amounts of other money saved:
Date:
Name and seal of applicant:
Name and seal of manager of House of Relaxation:
To: Officer in Charge, MANILA Sector Line of Communications Duties:

---

7. Form No. 7.

Request for permission to replace hostesses (geisha and waitresses) and others:
I hereby submit this request for permission to replace the following geisha, waitresses and others.

1. Persons:

Name	Date Birth	Sex	Professional Name	Home Residence	Present Residence	Position

2. Reasons:
3. Replacements:
Name, present residence, home residence:
Date:
Name and seal of manager:
To: Officer in Charge, MANILA Sector Line of Communications Duties:

Inconvenient and Uncomfortable

According to other U.S. military records, brothels for Japanese soldiers existed in other areas of the Philippine islands:

> (3) TACLOBAN. Portion of a bound mimeograph file, the section being entitled "TACLOBAN Brothel Regulations," undated, issued by MATSUNAGA Force, owner and unit not stated:
>
> 1. These regulations set down the provisions for the operation of brothels in TACLOBAN.
> 2. Places called 'Brothels' in these regulations are special brothels operated with Filipino women [licensed prostitutes].[17]

Judging from the information above, it appears that certain brothels included Filipino women.

> 3. The commanding officer and the adjutant of the garrison unit will have control over the supervision and direction of the brothels, and they will have Japanese associations operate them.[18]

Here, the supervision of the brothels is noted to be an explicit function of the Japanese military in Tacloban. As for the "Japanese associations" assuming the operation of the brothels, they are not defined in these sections, and the term calls for further research.

---

17 Ibid., p.14.

18 Ibid.

> 6. Those who operate the brothels must observe strictly the following provisions:
> a. Cleanliness and neatness of bedding, as well as its disinfection by sunlight.
> b. Perfection of facilities for prophylaxis by washing.
> c. Prohibition of added operation of food and drink shops.
> d. Prevention of indulgence by those not using a condom.
> e. Prohibition of activity by diseased women.
> f. Prevention of activity other than as regulated.
> g. Reporting by those operating the brothels to the adjutant on daily business conditions.[19]

These provisions indicate that the brothels were designed to be a well-regulated business enterprise placing emphasis on health and safety of the employees (i.e., the comfort women) and the soldiers, and any doubt as to such intent will be dispelled by this provision:

> 7. Those who intend to make use of the brothels must observe strictly the following provisions:
> d. There will not be any acts of violence or coercion either against the women in the brothels or against the operators of the brothels.[20]

---

19 Ibid.

20 Ibid.

Inconvenient and Uncomfortable 35

In addition to Tacloban, the U.S. military reports mention Burauen as another location on the Philippine islands where brothels existed:

> (4) BURAUEN. Portion of a bound handwritten and mimeographed file, the extract being entitled "Brothel Regulations", dated August 1944, issued by BURAUEN Sector Brothel, reproduced by 114 Airfield Battalion:
> 1. This brothel is opening in BURAUEN Town under the supervision of the TACLOBAN Sector Air Sector Commanding Officer.
> 2. Use of the brothel is limited to military personnel or Army civilian employees of air and related forces who have both medical certificates issued by the various forces and contraceptives. However, requests for the use of the brothel by ground troops of this sector can be granted after consultation by the committee upon receipt of an authorization from the sector commanding officer.[21]

Another U.S. military report identifies comfort women of Japanese and Korean stock as well as those of Spanish-Filipino ancestry run by local civilians in Manila:

> Brothels in PI – MANILA. Some were under Army jurisdiction. Others run by civilians were out of bounds, and MPs [military police] who tried to keep soldiers away, frequented these places themselves. Girls at civilian houses were usually half caste

---

21 Ibid., p.16.

SPANISH-FILIPINOS and prices YEN 10-20. Those at Army controlled houses were YEN 2-3 with JAP and KOREAN girls. Despite the differences in prices civilian houses were more popular, as they were less crowded.[22]

In view of these official U.S. military reports, an argument can be made that comfort women from Japan and Korea, the latter being part of the Japanese Empire at the time, worked at brothels in the Philippines under military supervision that enforced strict guidelines for the business operations along with the soldiers' code of conduct when visiting brothels. Moreover, certain brothels with Filipino licensed prostitutes appear to have been run by the Japanese military itself, but others outside of its jurisdiction owned by the locals existed and were actually destinations for certain men even though it went against policy. Given all the rules and regulations established by the Japanese military for a military-sanctioned brothel, from submission of documents such as business plans and affidavits required from the business applicant to encouraging the women to save money from their earnings, the tragic story of Maria Henson and others who shared similar experiences can be objectively deemed cases of wartime rape and violence while in captivity, not examples

---

[22] Allied Translator and Interpreter Section (ATIS) South West Pacific Area, Interrogation Report No. 573, Jan. 23, 1945, p.15.

within the realm of a meticulously designed and structured comfort women system by the Japanese Imperial Army.[23]

The description of Henson's experience in her autobiography, specifically being confined in a garrison compound or its vicinity where soldiers guarded the premises (without any established regulations to be followed), was "quite different from the typical comfort station in other parts of Asia, which in most cases was a facility completely separate from the barracks and managed by a Japanese or Korean civilian proprietor under the supervision of the military authorities."[24]

Furthermore, Henson ultimately escaped from her captors owing to a guerrilla attack on the barracks where she was being imprisoned by Japanese soldiers, ending her nine-month-long ordeal of April 1943 to January 1944.[25] Other Filipinas imprisoned and abused in a similar manner were held captive for up to several months.[26] In contrast, the majority of women labored at the comfort stations for a much longer period, typically ranging from a few years to more extended terms.

In order to validate the element of an institutionalized, systematic abduction, forcible recruitment, or conscription to characterize Japan's comfort women system, the scope of

---

23 The Japanese military tribunal in the Philippines had handed down nineteen criminal convictions by Jan. 1941. The Tokyo Trial delivered other guilty verdicts. Hata, Ikuhiko, *Ianfu to Senjō no Sei* (Comfort Women and Sexuality on the Battlefield), Shinchōsha Publishing Co., Ltd., Tokyo, (1999), p.377.

24 Henson, xvi.

25 Yoshimi, Yoshiaki, *Comfort Women: Sexual Slavery in the Japanese Military During World War II*, Columbia University Press, New York, (2000), p.145.

26 Ibid., p.194.

the analysis must go well beyond one territory (or nation) or a single ethnic population. Thus, the examination shall turn to other territories where the Japanese military was present.

B. Illegal Forcible Roundup: Semarang Case in the Dutch East Indies

The initial Japanese attack launched on the Dutch East Indies in January of 1942 led to the occupation of two islands, Borneo and Celebes. On March 1, 1942, Japanese troops landed on Java, the main island of the Dutch East Indies, forcing capitulation a week later.[1] Japan's 16th Army took over administrative control over the island of Java, and the Supreme Command of the 7th Army in Singapore, which fell directly under the authority of the government in Tokyo, was responsible for the regions including Java.[2]

The autobiography by Jan Ruff-O'Herne, a victim of sexual abuse and violence at a military brothel in Semarang, Dutch East Indies (present-day Indonesia) during World War II preceded Mary Henson's by two years. Ruff-O'Herne's *50 Years of Silence* was published in 1994, recounting her experience in Semarang on the island of Java in 1944.[3]

Often referred to as the Semarang Incident, the Japanese military's apparent forcible taking of women from prisoner-of-war camps that included Ruff-O'Herne, is regarded as **the only documentary evidence** that deals with the recruiting methods by the Japanese military in addition to the total

---

1 Poelgeest, Bart van. Report of a Study of Dutch Government Documents on the Forced Prostitution of Dutch Women in the Dutch East Indies during the Japanese Occupation, Unofficial Trans. 1994, (hereinafter "Poelgeest Translation"), p.3. (www.awf.or.jp/pdf/0205.pdf)

2 Ibid.

3 Soh, p.46.

number of women involved.[4] After the conclusion of World War II, the Temporary War Tribunal at Batavia (present-day Jakarta, Indonesia) prosecuted the individuals involved for 'Class B and C'[5] war crimes.[6]

While the Dutch government has sealed the details of the case involving Dutch and Eurasian women forced into prostitution until 2025[7], it released a report entitled "Report of a Study of Dutch Government Documents on the Forced Prostitution of Dutch Women in the Dutch East Indies during the Japanese Occupation" by Bart van Poelgeest (hereinafter "Poelgeest Report"). Together with what has been published as Court Documents Concerning the Case of the Semarang Comfort Stations, the summary of what transpired is as follows:

---

4 Ibid., p.20.

5 "When World War II ended in Asia, the consuming sentiments of the victorious Allies were hatred and hope; and the tangle of these emotions was nowhere made more apparent than in the war-crimes trials the victors conducted. The atrocities Japanese forces had committed in all theaters provoked a fierce desire for vengeance, and it was taken for granted that harsh punishment would be meted out to those found guilty of violating the established rules and conventions governing conduct of war. In formal terms, such 'conventional' atrocities, or 'crimes against humanity' more broadly defined, were identified as 'Class B' war crimes; the planning, ordering, authorization, or failure to prevent such transgressions at higher levels in the command structure were categorized as 'Class C' crimes." In practice, the two were often confused and it became common to refer to 'B/C' war crimes." Dower, John W., *Embracing Defeat: Japan in the Wake of World War II*, W. W. Norton & Co., New York, (1999), p.443.

6 Yoshimi, p.163.

7 Hicks, George, *The Comfort Women*, W.W. Norton & Company, New York, (1994), p.168.

In January 1944, a major of the Officer Candidate Corps (army cadet academy) of the Southern Army became the person in charge to set up new comfort stations (military brothels) in the district capital of Semarang located in the central area of Java. This Officer Candidate Corps of the Southern Army reported to the 16th Army Headquarters in Jakarta (known as Batavia until 1949).[8]

After being requested to set up comfort stations by the administrator of Semarang, the major of the Officer Candidate Corps sought permission from the 16th Army Headquarters to seek out women from the internment camps. During the post-WWII Temporary War Tribunal at Batavia, he testified that he had been informed by the officer who would become commander of the internment camps in Java that "it would be wise to have the women who consented (to become comfort women) write notes to that effect, so there won't be problems afterward." In another testimony by an officer who submitted the proposal to establish comfort stations and received the proper authorization, the Army Headquarters unequivocally informed him to "take special care that only freely consenting people were employed at the comfort station."[9]

Unfortunately, these orders were ignored, and the officers in charge, along with police and comfort station operators, began to forcibly round up young women from the internment camps. However, the leaders at several of the camps "put up so much opposition that the Japanese abandoned their attempts" after their motive to gather the women became

---

8 Yoshimi, p.164.

9 Ibid., pp.164-165.

apparent, yet approximately 35 of them were transported from these four camps:

> Halmahera – of the eleven women were gathered and taken away, three were sent home because of illness. A sixteen-year-old girl was also sent back for being too young. The court findings confirm eight women having been rounded up.
> Ambarawa (camp numbers 6 and 9; referred to nos. 4 and 6 by Batavia military court) – after fierce resistance by the women, about eighteen were taken away. The court found seventeen to have been rounded up.
> Gedangan – forced rounding up was halted after "fierce resistance," leading to tens of women reputed to have been prostitutes "consenting" to be transported. Several of these women were sent back to the camp shortly afterwards.[10]

The Temporary War Tribunal at Batavia concluded that 25 women were taken from Halmahera and Ambarawa camps and forced to engage in prostitution.[11]

The women were kept at four comfort stations from March 1 but were released about two months later when the 16th Army Headquarters ordered the closure of them. The abrupt shutdown of the brothels came about after a protest by a local leader to a colonel from Tokyo Army Headquarters who promptly reported to three command posts about the forcible nature of recruiting: the Ministry of War, the South Army

---

10 Ibid., pp.165-166.

11 Ibid., p.166.

Headquarters in Tokyo; the 7th Area Army Headquarters in Singapore (established in March 1944); and the 16th Army Headquarters in Jakarta. The 16th Army Headquarters immediately ordered the brothels to be closed down. The colonel who made the report belonged to the Ministry of War's Prisoner of War Department and had been on a tour to inspect the conditions of the civilian and prisoner-of-war camps.[12]

On March 24, 1948, the Temporary War Tribunal found eleven men guilty: seven officers and four civilian military employees who operated the comfort stations. The convictions included rounding up of women for the purpose of forced prostitution, forcing to engage in prostitution, and rape – the comfort stations being locations for rape was acknowledged by the court. Of the thirteen defendants, sentences ranged from two to 20 years, with one death penalty (a major primarily in charge of establishing comfort stations) and two were found not guilty. An officer who had worked with a commander of the Officer Candidate Corps committed suicide before he could be brought to trial.[13]

The Poelgeest Report provides additional circumstantial information that led to the Semarang Incident:

> Neither the government in Tokyo nor the supreme command of the 7th army issued general regulations or instructions with regard to the establishment of military brothels in the former Dutch East Indies.[14]

---

12 Ibid., p.171.

13 Ibid., pp.171-173.

14 Poelgeest Translation, pp. 3-4.

The above reveals the absence of any basic organizational guidelines coming from military high command in establishing comfort stations in the Dutch East Indies, and the following describes the extent of the decision-making at the local level:

> In practice, it was the local military commanders who had to draw up regulations on the establishment of military brothels in their territory. The chief of staff of the 16th army on Java and thus head of the military administration there decided that a license was required for the establishment of a military brothel. A license was issued only if certain conditions were met, relating to, for example, regular medical check-ups and payment. A further precondition was that the women working in the brothels had to do so voluntarily; according to the regulations, a license would only be issued if the women involved signed a statement to the effect that they were providing their services voluntarily. Within the organization of the 16th army, the officer in charge of the commissariat (the "heitan" officer) was responsible for issuing these licenses and for ensuring observance of the conditions under which they were issued.[15]

Local military authorities took the initiative to implement strict requirements in relation to the establishment of and how the women qualified to join the comfort stations. Forcible recruitment and forced prostitution were clearly

---

15 Ibid., p.4. Corrections made for typos in the original text.

against military policy, and the ethnicities of the women are also mentioned:

> Apart from women of Japanese and Korean origin, the women recruited for the Japanese military brothels in the Dutch East Indies came from three groups, i.e. Indonesian women, European women living in the internment camps, and European women living outside the camps.[16]

After outlining the three-and-a-half year period of the Japanese occupation in regards to comfort stations and the women involved, the Poelgeest Report makes this assessment:

> The study shows that in recruiting European women for their military brothels in the Dutch East Indies, the Japanese occupiers used force in some cases. Of the two hundred to three hundred European women working in these brothels, 65 were most certainly forced into prostitution.[17]

The breakdown of 65 women "most certainly forced into prostitution" includes those transferred from the Muntilan camp and others near Semarang[18], though the Temporary War Tribunal did not hand down additional guilty verdicts.

The findings of the Poelgeest Report demonstrate that: a) no supreme command from Japan's military headquarters ordered a systematic seizure of women for the purpose of

---

16 Ibid.

17 Ibid., p.2.

18 Ibid., p.18.

forced prostitution; b) local military authorities in Semarang suggested licenses for setting up comfort stations and only have women who voluntarily agreed to the work involved; and c) violations of such local policy still occurred, resulting in human rights violations. In order to explore the circumstances of other parts of the Dutch territory Japan took over during WWII, the Netherlands East Indies Forces Intelligence Service (NEFIS) provides information gathered after evacuating from the islands and setting up a unit in Australia. Although the NEFIS reports are comprised of information taken from third parties, they intimate anything but an organized, systematic forcible recruitment of women all over the Japanese-occupied East Indies.

NEFIS Report, dated 6 Dec 44, Compilation of NEFIS Interrogation Report Nos. 534, 552, 567, 568, 579, 586, 587, 588, and 592:

> XIII. General. Prostitution: A brothel was located in... having as its inmates a very large number of Indonesian girls and women, for the exclusive use of Japanese military personnel. They were very carefully selected from what would appear to be a number of willing applicants. No girl or women who had given birth of a child was eligible. Those selected received a premium of 300 guilders and an outfit of fine clothing of a desirable type.[19]

NEFIS Report, dated 29 Oct 44, Compilations of NEFIS Interrogation Report Nos. 366-378, 404-407, and 410-417:

---

19 Miyamoto, Archie, *Wartime Military Records on Comfort Women: Compilation of U.S./Allied/Dutch/Japanese Military Documents*, (2018), p.29.

> Interrogation of Indonesians. Prostitution: "During '43 at Solo (Mid-Java) – A Javanese [native of Java] who lived in Mid-Java selected girls for prostitution for use by Japanese troops. During '43, at Solo (mid-Java) a Chinese was given a permit to use the Russche Hotel for prostitutes for Japanese officers. He selected girls from the village with the help of the assistant village chief offering them work for money. One informant from Amboebe (E Java) said village girls were selected for restaurants and for prostitution.[20]

NEFIS Interrogation Report No. 422, dated 23 Oct 43:

> Interrogation of Indonesian. Sumatra. Prostitution. At Medan, officers have access to Japanese women brought from Japan. Others have access to Indonesian women.[21]

NEFIS Report, dated 23 Mar 45, Compilation of Reports Nos. 1235-1238:

> Interrogation of Indonesian. Prostitution, Tarakan, NE Borneo. About 50 Japanese women were housed near a hospital at 'Ladang'.[22]

NEFIS Interrogation Report No. 1252, dated 10 May 45:

---

20 Ibid., p.30.
21 Ibid., p.32.
22 Ibid., p.31.

Interrogation of Indonesian school teacher. Prostitution in N. Celebes. There were two houses of prostitution, one for officers with 30 women, one for NCO/men with 50 women. Women were from various locales. **They received monthly salaries, kept all the money given by clients.** Clothing, etc, were provided. The women had to pass physical exams, a regular check by a physician. In the event of disease, they were treated at hospital, then sent home. They were at liberty to leave the brothels for fixed periods.[23]

These reports indicate that Japanese women disembarked on the occupied islands of the Dutch East Indies in the same manner they did in other parts of the South Pacific including Rabaul and the Philippines. Yet, women were sought out from the local populace as well, and while it is extremely difficult to conclude how much authority the Japanese military exercised over the brothels, civilian operators apparently existed, and not all of them were Japanese. Since the presence of Korean women has already been confirmed in Rabaul and the Philippines, a substantive examination on the recruiting of women on the Korean Peninsula, Japan's annexed territory (not a battleground in the Pacific) must be undertaken. Furthermore, the additional role often taken by those who engaged in recruiting of the women will be explored in the following section.

---

23 Ibid.

C. Japan's Annexed Territory: The Korean Peninsula

The previous sections dealt with the Philippines and the Dutch East Indies, two newly occupied enemy territories that remained battleground areas in Southeast Asia until the Japanese military was either defeated or forced to retreat by the Allied Forces. In the case of Korea, an annexed territory of Japan since 1910, a very different state of affairs manifests itself with respect to its comfort women experience.

After failed negotiations between Russia and Japan, the two nations that exercised "direct power" in Korean affairs throughout the 1890s than any other foreign empire, the Russo-Japanese War broke out at Port Arthur in February of 1904.[1] With President Theodore Roosevelt mediating the Treaty of Portsmouth to end hostilities eighteen months later, Japan emerged as Korea's new protectorate. On August 29, 1910, a week after the Treaty of Annexation had been entered into by Japan and Korea, Sunjong, the mentally-retarded son and successor to King Kojong (or Gojong), yielded his throne, effectively making Korea a colony, thereby concluding the Choson (or Joseon) dynasty which lasted for over five centuries.[2]

Opposing views of the annexation period of Korea by Japan have been expounded by historians, with an overwhelming majority expressing one perspective in the past several decades. That said, the economic benefits by the industrial development during the annexation period can be confirmed

---

1 Cumings, Bruce, *Korea's Place in the Sun,* W.W. Norton & Company, New York, (1997), p.141.

2 Ibid., p.145.

by data[3], but below is a relatively concise assessment given by Professor Bruce Cumings:

> Japan held Korea tightly, watched it closely, and pursued an organized, architectonic colonialism in which the planner and administrator was the model, not the swashbuckling conqueror; the strong, highly centralized colonial state mimicked the role that the Japanese state had come to play in Japan – intervening in the economy, creating markets, spawning new industries, suppressing dissent. Politically, Koreans could barely breathe, but economically there was significant, if unevenly distributed growth. Agricultural output rose substantially in the 1920s, and a hothouse industrialization took root in the 1930s. Growth rates in the Korean economy often outstripped those in Japan itself; recent research has suggested an annual growth rate for Korea of 3.57 percent in the period 1911-38, a rate of 3.36 percent for Japan itself.[4]

Perhaps the most cited U.S. military document on the issue of Japan's comfort women is the U.S. Office of War Information, Japanese Prisoner of War Interrogation Report No. 49 (hereinafter referred to as "U.S. Interrogation Report No. 49"). Based on information collected from a group of 20 captured Korean comfort women near Myitkyina, Burma (present-day Myanmar) in 1944, the report covers a wide range

---

3 For instance, Professor Alleyne Ireland's *The New Korea* published in 1926 presents various data.

4 Cumings, p.148.

of topics including the women's pay and living conditions, their personality, and of course, how they were recruited.[5]

After defining the comfort women as "nothing more than a prostitute or "professional camp follower" attached to the Japanese Army for the benefit of the soldiers," the report goes on to explain that Japanese agents enlisted young Korean women in early May of 1942 for "comfort service" in parts of Southeast Asia which were recently conquered by Japanese forces.[6]

In the Recruiting section, it reads:

> The nature of this "service" was not specified but it was assumed to be work connected with visiting the wounded in hospitals, rolling bandages, and generally making the soldiers happy. The inducement used by these agents was plenty of money, an opportunity to pay off the family debts, easy work, and the prospect of a new life in a new land, Singapore. On the basis of these false representations many girls enlisted for overseas duty and were rewarded with an advance of a few hundred yen.[7]

---

[5] United States Office of War Information Psychological Warfare Team Attached to U.S. Army Forces India-Burma Theater, APO 689, Japanese Prisoner of War Interrogation Report No. 49," Oct. 1, 1944 (hereinafter "U.S. Office of War Information, Interrogation Report No. 49"), pp.1-6. (http://www.exordio.com/1939-1945/codex/Documentos/report-49-USA-orig.html) *Appendix "A" not shown.

[6] Ibid.

[7] Ibid.

Put in perspective, the monthly salary of an enlisted soldier was between 6 and 10 yen[8], and that of a sergeant between 23 and 30 yen.[9]

As for the contractual obligation involved, they were bound to the Japanese Army regulations and also to work for the "house master" between six months to a year, a period that depended "on the family debt for which they were advanced money."[10] The report states the average age of these "comfort girls" to be about 25 years old, and they were part of the approximately 800 who "were recruited in this manner and they landed with their Japanese "house master" at Rangoon around August 20, 1942."[11]

At the end of this report, an Appendix provides the list of the 20 women and their Japanese agent, and recently a U.S. war veteran pointed out that this agent couple came from present-day Seoul, South Korea.[12] The address (place of origin) for Mr. and Mrs. Kitamura reads 'Keikido, Keijo,' as it does for two of the women, Kin Tonhi and Ha Tonyo.[13]

Thus, the Japanese agents the report refers to were ethnic Koreans having Japanese citizenship, for Korea was an annexed territory of Japan at that time. As citizens of Japan, many residents of the Korean Peninsula adopted Japanese names. Consequently, not only does this U.S. Interrogation Report No. 49 explicitly indicate deception as a method to recruit comfort women of Korean ancestry, it also reveals

---

8 Soh, p.140.

9 Hata, p.394.

10 Miyamoto, pp.12-14.

11 U.S. Office of War Information, Interrogation Report No. 49, pp.1-2.

12 Miyamoto, p.13.

13 Ibid., Appendix "A."

the perpetrators of such deceptive recruiting as members of the same ethnicity. This may be quite logical as Korean was their native tongue, and as compatriots on the peninsula, these agents (the recruiters also happened to be proprietors in this case, which was quite common) shared the same customs and traditions that existed long before the Japanese annexation in 1910.

UNITED STATES OFFICE OF WAR INFORMATION
Psychological Warfare Team
Attached to U.S. Army Forces India-Burma Theater.
APO 689

Japanese Prisoner of War Interrogation Report No. 49.	Place interrogated: Date interrogated: Date of Report: By:	Ledo Stockade Aug. 20 - Sept.10, 1944 October 1, 1944 T/3 Alex Yorichi

Prisoners: Date of Capture: Date of Arrival at Stockade:	20 Korean Comfort Girls August 10, 1944 August 15, 1944

PREFACE:

This report is based on the information obtained from the interrogation of twenty Korean "comfort girls" and two Japanese civilians captured around the tenth of August, 1944 in the mopping up operations after the fall of Myitkyina in Burma.

The report shows how the Japanese recruited these Korean "comfort girls", the conditions under which they lived and worked, their relations with and reaction to the Japanese soldier, and their understanding of the military situation.

A "comfort girl" is nothing more than a prostitute or "professional camp follower" attached to the Japanese Army for the benefit of the soldiers. The word "comfort girl" is peculiar to the Japanese. Other reports show the "comfort girls" have been found wherever it was necessary for the Japanese Army to fight. This report however deals only with the Korean "comfort girls" recruited by the Japanese and attached to their Army in Burma. The Japanese are reported to have shipped some 703 of these girls to Burma in 1942.

RECRUITING:

Early in May of 1942 Japanese agents arrived in Korea for the purpose of enlisting Korean girls for "comfort service" in newly conquered Japanese territories in Southeast Asia. The nature of this "service" was not specified but it was assumed to be work connected with visiting the wounded in hospitals, rolling bandages, and generally making the soldiers happy. The inducement used by these agents was plenty of money, an opportunity to pay off the family debts, easy work, and the prospect of a new life in a new land - Singapore. On the basis of these false representations many girls enlisted for overseas duty and were rewarded with an advance of a few hundred yen.

The majority of the girls were ignorant and uneducated, although a few had been connected with "oldest profession on earth" before. The contract they signed bound them to Army regulations and to work for the "house master" for a period of from six months to a year depending on the family debt for which they were advanced

APPENDIX "A"

Following are the names of the twenty Korean "comfort girls" and the two Japanese civilians interrogated to obtain the information used in this report. The Korean names are phoneticised.

	Name	Age	Address
1.	Shin Jyun Nimi	21	Keishonando, Shinshu
2.	Kak Yonja	28	" Sensenpo, Yunwi
3.	Pen Yonja	26	" Shinshu
4.	Chinja Chunto	21	Keishohokudo, Taikyu
5.	Chun Yonja	27	Keishonando, Shinshu
6.	Kim Monju	25	Keishohokudo, Taikyu
7.	Kim Youja	19	" "
8.	Kim Kenja	25	Keishonando, Hosan
9.	Kim Senni	21	" Kunboku
10.	Kim Kun Sun	22	" Taikyu
11.	Kim Chongi	26	" Shinshu
12.	Pe Kija	27	" "
13.	Chun Punyi	21	" Keisan Nan, Koyosan Kura
14.	Koko Sunyi	21	" Konyo, Sokiboku Do, Kyu Ruri
15.	Yon Muji	31	Heiannando, Heijo
16.	Opu Ni	20	" "
17.	Kim Tonhi	20	Keikido, Keijo
18.	Ha Tonyo	21	" "
19.	Oki Song	20	Keishohokudo, Taikyu
20.	Kim Guptoge	21	Zenranando, Koshu

Japanese Civilians:

| 1. | Kitamura, Tomiko | 38 | Keikido, Keijo |
| 2. | " Eibun | 41 | " " |

ND-97
(7)

In another U.S. military document, information on five captured ethnic Korean women identified as prostitutes in Luzon, Philippines includes the following:

> The families of all the women were extremely poor and in order to save their families the expense of caring for them and to get some money they were sold to a Geisha House in KOREA. They were sent to TAICHU City, FORMOSA [present-day Taichung, Taiwan] and placed in the employ of the Army.[14]

In Professor C. Sarah Soh's groundbreaking book *The Comfort Women*, countless statements of former Korean comfort women are quoted, including personal interviews she conducted as part of her extensive research. As a scholar fluent in English, Japanese, and Korean who has interviewed over 100 former comfort women, her work offers the multifaceted and divergent circumstances involving the recruiting process of the women. In this bold, thought-provoking 2008 publication that features her research since 1995, she declares from the outset that:

> Whereas some Korean survivors stated having been kidnapped, others revealed that they were "sold" to human traffickers by their indigent parents. In fact, compatriot "entrepreneurs" – men and women from colonial Korea who not only procured girls and women

---

14 Headquarters U.S. I Corps, 163d Language Detachment Report No. 163LD-I 0223 "Combined Enemy Alien Preliminary Interrogation Report", May 21, 1945.

for the Japanese army but also, in many cases, managed or ran comfort stations–lured the majority of them.[15]

Of the elderly Korean women survivors who have come out in public since 1991, only the very few had received formal education, and the vast majority shared impoverished family backgrounds.[16] According to Soh's findings, women such as Yi Sun-ok, Pae Chok-kan, and Mun Pil-gi, were approached by a Korean individual (usually male but sometimes female) regarding an opportunity to earn money (typically at some factory), only to be tricked and delivered to comfort stations outside of Korea. Kim Sun-ok had been sold four times by her parents from the tender age of seven, and as soon as she returned to her hometown of Pyongyang after paying off her debt of 500 won, "procurers began showing up" at her parents' house.[17] Despite her entreaties not to sell her again, this time to Manchuria, her father explained, "...Go this one time. They promised to send you to a factory, which should be a good thing."[18] Yi Sang-ok joined other young women who had been sold by their parents, expecting to work at a factory in Japan – however, these women's dreams were shattered after finding themselves taken to a Korean couple in Pusan who owned a brothel.[19]

Among the South Korean survivors, some have given varying accounts of their story as comfort women, particularly

---

15 Soh, pp.3-4.

16 Ibid., pp.59-60.

17 Ibid., p.11.

18 Ibid.

19 Ibid., pp.86-87.

with respect to how they were recruited.[20] Soh utilizes the term 'testimonial narrative' when referring to the women's personal accounts that have been published[21] (as opposed to 'testimony,' which has a legalistic meaning as a primary definition[22]), and the subsequent references of the women's stories will be referred to as such.

Kim Kun-ja (also transliterated as Kim Koon-ja), one of the three former comfort women who gave testimonies before the U.S. House of Representatives subcommittee that led to the unanimous passage of House Resolution 121 in 2007, dramatized her account by claiming that she had been "captured" in front of the railroad station and taken away to China in a train full of other women and soldiers.[23] In her original testimonial narrative published in 1999, however, she declares that her foster father "sold" her.[24] In October 2003, Kim reportedly stated in an interview that she "hated the father more than the Japanese military."[25]

---

20 Ibid., p.99.

21 Ibid., p.79.

22 Evidence given by a competent witness under oath or affirmation; as distinguished from evidence derived from writings, and other sources. Black's Law Dictionary, Sixth Edition by the Publisher's Editorial Staff, West Publishing Co., St. Paul, MN, (1990), p.1476.

1 a : a solemn declaration usually made orally by a witness under oath in response to interrogation by a lawyer or authorized public official. (https://www.merriam-webster.com/dictionary/testimony)

23 Soh, p.101.

24 Ibid.

25 Ibid.

Kim Hak-sun, the first Korean ever to publicly appear to divulge her past as having been a comfort woman for the Japanese military in December 1991, has offered conflicting testimonial narratives including the recruiting process:

> a) as one of the plaintiffs in the 1991 class-action lawsuit heard by Tokyo District Court, she asserted that after being trained to become *kisaeng* (the *geisha* equivalent in Korea), her foster father took her along with other young women to a small village called Cholpyokjin (Tiebizhen in Chinese) and left them there;[26]
>
> b) in the 1993 published version, she was separated from her foster father by the Japanese military after arriving in Beijing, forcibly taken to a house apparently being operated as a comfort station;[27]
>
> c) according to an original unpublished account Professor Soh personally learned during her research, Kim's foster father had actually managed the comfort station until he later vanished.[28]

In Soh's book, more information is revealed on the foster father - that Kim had been sold to him by her mother, and that he gave her formal *kisaeng* training after changing her name. Moreover, this foster father chose to find work for her in China because at seventeen, she was still a minor and unable to work as a *kisaeng* in Korea.[29] Needless to say, the

---

26 Ibid., p.127.

27 Ibid.

28 Ibid.

29 Ibid., p.128.

version of Kim's testimonial narrative promoted by Korean activists leaves out the role of the foster father having been the comfort station manager.[30]

As can be seen by these examples, Soh's extensive study "documents the collective complicity of Korean collaborators"[31] which, tragically, was in actuality a continuation of what had transpired on the Korean Peninsula years before Japan's comfort women system was implemented. As Japan occupied parts of China after the Sino-Japanese War (1894-1895), the 1920s saw a migration of many working-class Korean women into China to work at brothels for the Japanese military.[32]

It has been estimated by Korean scholar Song Youn-ok that by the mid-1920s, 5,000 to 6,000 brokers of brothels existed in Seoul alone, and at times, deceptive means of recruitment or even outright abduction took place.[33] According to an annual statistical data by the Government-General of Korea that recorded the number of licensed prostitutes since 1910, the total number of Japanese sexual laborers on the Korean Peninsula was not surpassed by their native counterparts until 1931 - in 1910, the data shows 4,091 Japanese licensed prostitutes and 1,193 Koreans. By 1931, there were 4,361 Japanese and 5,073 Korean prostitutes, and in 1942, 7,942

---

30 Yi, J. (Jan. 31, 2018) Confronting Korea's Censored Discourse on Comfort Women. The Diplomat. (https://thediplomat.com/2018/01/confronting-koreas-censored-discourse-on-comfort-women/)

31 Soh, xiv.

32 Allen, Chizuko, "The Paradigm that Supports the Korean Comfort Women Redress Movement." Japan Forum for Strategic Studies, vol. 68, 2016, p.39.

33 Ibid., pp.39-40.

were Korean as opposed to 3,810 Japanese.[34] Such data could be interpreted in different ways, but evidently not until the early 1930s did licensed Korean laborers outnumber the Japanese on the peninsula.

The unfortunate reality of deception utilized in the recruitment of sexual labor probably existed as long as 'the world's oldest profession' itself. Prostitution was legal in Japan as well as in the annexed territory of Korea, with the minimum age requirement of licensed prostitutes at eighteen and seventeen, respectively.[35] Efforts by the Japanese police to thwart human trafficking in Korea have been documented[36], as penal codes mirrored those in Japan proper. Korean natives made up roughly half of the police personnel[37], some served as police chiefs, and they presided as magistrates in most counties on the peninsula.[38]

---

34 Hata, p.41.

35 Soh, p.9.

36 For examples, refer to website "Comfort Women by Scholars in English": http://scholarsinenglish.blogspot.com/2014/10/korean-newspaper-articles-from-1930s.html

37 Cumings, p.178.

38 In 1945, 198 out of 219 county magistrates were Korean natives. Hata, p.379.

1939.03.28 동아일보
50여 처녀가 조선인 인신매매단에 걸려서 북지, 만주에 창기로 팔림.
일본경찰이 구해줌.
March 28, 1939 Donga Ilbo
Over 50 women were deceived by a Korean trafficker (Bae Jang-eon 배장언)
and sent to Northern China & Manchuria.
He was arrested and the women were rescued by Japanese policemen.

1933.06.30 동아일보
노상에서 소녀를 유인하여 납치,
추업중인(매춘포주)에게 매도, 범인은 박명동과 이성녀
June 30, 1933 Donga Ilbo
A girl was kidnapped from the street by
Korean traffickers (Park Myeong-dong & Lee Seong-nyeo)

Inconvenient and Uncomfortable

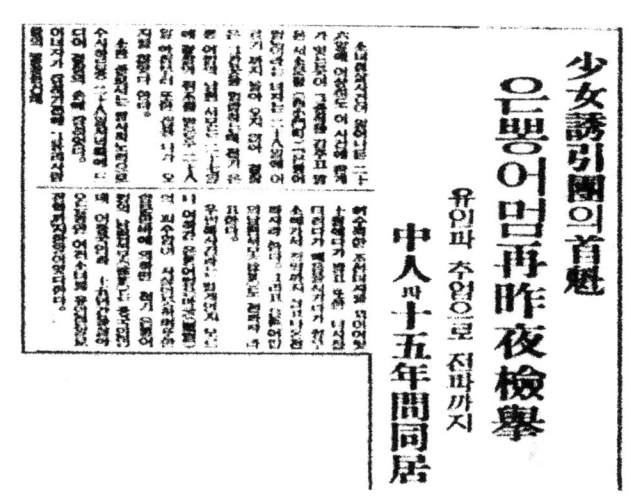

1933.07.01 동아일보
소녀유인단의 수괴 은뽕어멈.
주로 어린 소녀들을 꾀어다가 매음굴에 팔아 먹던 악녀였는데,
일본경찰이 검거함.
July 1, 1933 Donga Ilbo
A leader of the Korean group that trafficked girls to
Korean comfort station owners was arrested last night.

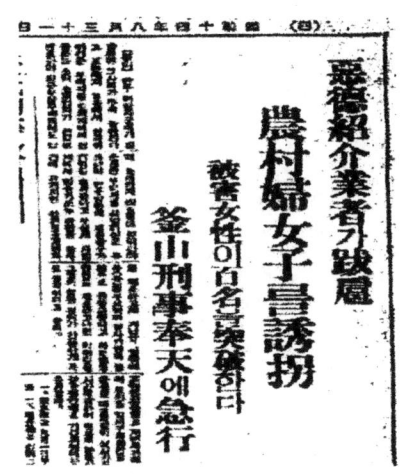

1939.08.31 동아일보
악덕소개업자가 발호,
이들이 유괴한 농촌부녀자의 수가 무려 100명 이상.
모두 일본경찰님들이 구출해내심.
August 31, 1939 Donga Ilbo
Over 100 women from farming villages were deceived
by Korean traffickers (Kim Ok-man 김옥만 & his family)
They were arrested and the women were rescued by Japanese policemen.

純眞한 農村處女
百餘名 誘引賣喫
西署에서 『二河允明』事件

1936.02.14 매일신보
조선인들이 여자 유인해서 창기로 팔아 먹는걸
일본경찰이 발견하고 검거함.
February 14, 1936 Maeil Shinbo
Korean traffickers who deceived and sold women
to Korean comfort station owners were arrested by police.

Similarly, pursuant to Penal Code Article 226, the police in Japan cracked down on traffickers scheming to send Japanese women overseas.[39] Records of such cases making news headlines and resulting in criminal sentences are documented.[40]

In 2017, police documents dealing with human traffickers in January 1938 were unearthed at a university in Japan. The documents involve three suspects who claimed to be agents of the military to transport women from Nagasaki to Shanghai, assuring the police "not to be suspicious."[41] They were charged for abduction as they "told unsuspecting women they would be paid well, fed, clothed and provided a place to stay as long as they comforted soldiers."[42]

What has been opined by, among others, a South Korean scholar further clouds the contention against the Japanese military: while some testimonial narratives involve forcible seizure of women, it is highly possible that agents and recruiters wore uniforms and were mistaken as soldiers.[43] However, even if certain soldiers had engaged in the forcible taking away of women, such cases should be deemed aberrations since the Korean Peninsula was not a battleground during the Pacific War, and not being a war zone, penal codes existed which, unless universal lawlessness had been

---

39 Hata, p.53.

40 Ibid., pp.53-54.

41 Kim, B. (August 13, 2017) 'Japanese Police Saw Sex Slave Mobilization as Crime', *The Korea Times* (English), Foreign Affairs. (http://www.koreatimes.co.kr/www/nation/2017/08/120_234653.html)

42 Ibid.

43 Park, Yu-ha, *Teikoku no Ianfu* (Comfort Women of the Empire), Asahi Shimbun Publications Inc., Tokyo, (2014), p.46.

prevalent, would have forced military personnel to think twice about seizing women at whim. The extent of Japanese military presence on the Korean Peninsula becomes another factor in carrying out systematic forcible taking of women, but as a matter of common sense, the 'needs' and 'behaviors' of soldiers must have greatly differed from those deployed in parts of Asia where tensions were constantly high owing to continuous combat.

For the prevailing narrative of an institutionalized, systematic abduction, forcible recruitment or conscription of women to have any validity on the Korean Peninsula, further analysis inevitably leads to how the comfort women redress movement first came about in South Korea and gradually emerged as an international human rights issue. The focus in the following section will be the development of Korea's redress movement that has greatly capitalized on what has been crystalized globally as Japan's comfort women paradigm.

D. The Paradigmatic Story of Systematic Forcible Recruitment by the Japanese Military

On December 6, 1991, Kim Hak-sun gave an emotional press conference in Tokyo by revealing herself in public as a former comfort woman for the Japanese military, the very first non-Japanese to do so. Yoshie Mihara (aka Suzuko Shirota) conducted a radio interview in 1986 with TBS, a major Japanese station, to discuss her story as a comfort woman and eventually a manager of a comfort station.[1] Kim's revelation as a former comfort woman caused political and diplomatic pandemonium in Japan and South Korea. Various pressure groups and the media including *Asahi Shimbun*, one of Japan's largest newspapers, forced the Japanese government to acknowledge then Imperial Japan's government to have had involvement in the comfort women system. *Asahi* was singularly instrumental by reporting on Professor Yoshiaki Yoshimi's *exposé* of documents that "clearly implicate the Japanese government in the establishment and maintenance" of Imperial Japan's military brothels.[2] On January 13, 1992, the government issued an apology that would be repeated four days later by then Prime Minister Miyazawa during a state visit in Seoul, South Korea.[3]

While the first report on the comfort women system based on an investigation by both Tokyo and Seoul was issued in July 1992[4], the issue gained strong traction in the international

---

1 Soh, p.198.

2 Ibid., p.44.

3 Ibid.

4 Ibid.

human rights community, resulting in numerous articles, reports, and recommendations by activists, scholars, and non-governmental organizations including the United Nations.

Jan Ruff-O'Herne published the first autobiography in 1994 followed by Maria Rosa Henson's two years later. Aside from these autobiographies by actual women survivors, legal specialists connected to international organizations such as the U.N. wrote reports with the emphasis on sexual slavery. ICJ (International Commission of Jurists) became the first multinational entity to publish a report on the issue by introducing the paradigmatic story of "forcible recruitment by the military," concluding that the women in the comfort stations went through "a "living hell" of beating, torture, and rape."[5] This "monolithic representation of the comfort system as sexual slavery"[6] has continued as the globally dominant paradigmatic story ever since, and with the transnational human rights activists playing a major role to advance such narrative, this comfort women paradigm became the *de facto* "transnational English-language template"[7] as we know it.

As this paradigmatic story spread across the world, it may have only been natural, if not indispensable for certain former comfort women to add dramatic, untruthful exaggerations to their original published stories "in order to live up to" the narrative of "forcible recruitment by the Japanese military."[8] Soh explains in her book that some other women either "have firmly refused to be further interviewed" since the initial investigation by the South Korean government for registration

---

5 Ibid., p.47.

6 Ibid.

7 Ibid., p.24.

8 Ibid., p.101.

purposes or remained silent for fear of accidental "speech errors" that would result in termination of welfare payments.[9]

Lee Yong-su (also transliterated as Yi Yong-su), a former comfort woman who has appeared in cities where statues and monuments were considered for installation[10] may be an exemplary choice to illustrate how the recruiting details have been revised to adapt to the paradigmatic story.

Her published testimonial narrative divulges her decision to leave home in the fall of 1944 with her friend Pun-sun at dawn as the latter quietly knocked on her window.[11] She describes what she wore and how delighted she was when receiving a red dress and leather shoes in a packet by a recruiter.[12] "I tiptoed out and furtively followed Pun-sun to leave home. Without letting my mother know, I simply left home by following my friend."[13] The subsequent statements she has made seem to sensationalize the notion of being "dragged away by the Japanese military during sleep" which undoubtedly correlates with the paradigmatic story of forcible recruitment by the Japanese military.[14] However, her original

---

9 Ibid.

10 Her most recent and celebrated appearance at the time of this writing was on Sept. 22, 2017 in San Francisco's opening ceremony of the comfort women statues. (http://www.foxnews.com/us/2017/09/22/san-francisco-unveils-memorial-to-wwii-comfort-women.html)

11 Soh, p.99.

12 Ibid., p.100.

13 Ibid., pp.99-100.

14 Ibid., p.100.

published testimonial narrative presents a determined young woman who desperately sought a better life.[15]

On February 15, 2007, Lee's testimony before the U.S. House of Representatives involved a downright abduction, that "she was sleeping at night" when a Japanese and a girl came, and "covering her mouth, dragged her away."[16] Amazingly, the written statement submitted by activists from South Korea on her behalf to the subcommittee in charge of the hearings proved essentially identical to her original published story:

> A few days later, Punsan knocked on my window early in the morning, and whispered to me to follow her quietly. I tip-toed out of the house after her. I left without telling my mother.[17]

Since the early 1990s, Lee has given many different statements[18] that range from how she was forcibly recruited (soldier/s used a sword, bayonet, pistol, etc.), incidents of physical violence inflicted by soldiers (including electric shocks), and how long she labored at a comfort station in Taiwan (in actuality she was there for less than a year). Along with Kim Kun-ja, the other Korean woman who

---

15　Ibid.

16　Ibid.

17　Protecting the Human Rights of Comfort Women, 2007: Hearing before the Subcomm. on Asia, the Pacific, and the Global Environment of the Comm. on Foreign Affairs House of Representatives, 110th Cong., 1st Sess. (2007), p.20 (23 of 95). (http://archives-republicans-foreignaffairs.house.gov/110/33317.pdf)

18　This link lists the many statements she has made over the years: https://docs.google.com/document/d/171fHdHD-xFU1g7-XAuuYVhR4wMwZ9VBwKVXPCu78riE/edit

testified before the U.S. House of Representatives, their original testimonial narratives that were published do not comport with the paradigmatic story of abduction or forcible recruitment by the Japanese military.

It has been inferred that the South Korean activists' rhetorical strategy to utilize 'forcible recruitment' was standardized since 1993, the year when a series of collections of survivors' testimonial narratives was published under the title *Kangjero Kkullyogan Chosonin Kunwianbudul* (Forcibly Dragged Away Korean Military Comfort Women).[19]

The only male historian of the research team that compiled the first volume of this project, Professor Ahn Byung-jik (also transliterated as An Byeong-jik), parted ways with the others after three years of joint research. He found the "members to be more interested in fighting against Japan than in learning about the historical facts."[20] After proclaiming that "no objective data existed on forcible recruitment of Korean women under Japanese rule" on a major TV network thirteen years later, Ahn became the object of relentless criticism in South Korea. While he did recognize the possibility of coercive recruitments, he was chastised for making a pro-Japan statement nonetheless.[21]

For many years, activists, scholars, and others supporting the comfort women redress movement have referred to Seiji Yoshida's 'confessional' books as a source to substantiate Japan's forcible recruitment of women. His books published in 1977 and 1983 offered detailed accounts of 'hunting' Korean women on Cheju (or Jeju) Island as a member of

---

19 Soh, p.102.

20 Ibid.

21 Ibid., p.103.

the civilian labor department in Shimonoseki, a port city in Yamaguchi Prefecture having ferryboats to the Korean island.[22] In his first work, he professed to have recruited 100 women and in the second publication 205 women in a week that sometimes involved physical force. His account also alleged soldiers sexually violating the conscripted women in a military warehouse, thereby greatly contributing to the paradigmatic story.[23]

From the outset, Yoshida's stories involving Korean comfort women recruitment raise certain questions. For one, as an annexed territory of Japan, all government matters including labor issues in Korea had been under the authority and jurisdiction of the Government-General of Korea, and having anyone from a domestic department in Japan proper engage in the mobilization of Korean residents defies logic.[24] Yoshida publicly claimed to have been a soldier earlier in his 'career' as a writer and activist on the comfort women issue, but he had never served in the Japanese military. Information on Yoshida's past, from his birth, use of several names, education, work history, to his reasons for serving a two-year sentence[25], is as elusive and inconsistent as the series of claims he made in 1992 with respect to the number of women he supposedly recruited:

22　Ibid., pp.152-153.
23　Ibid., p.153.
24　Hata, p.244.
25　Ibid., p.245.

950 - January 23 reported by *Asahi Shimbun*;[26]

at least 1,000 – January 26 by *Akahata*, Japan's Communist newspaper;[27]

950 per his recollection but 2,000 according to his subordinates – March 13 and 16 during interview by Prof. Ikuhiko Hata;[28]

6,000 (including male laborers) – May 25 by *Asahi Shimbun*;[29]

2,000 – August 8 by *New York Times*;[30]

When Professor Ikuhiko Hata, Japan's prominent historian and critic of the comfort women redress movement, conducted research on Cheju Island, he discovered a review of Yoshida's book by reporter Ho Yong-son of *Cheju Sinmum* in 1989.[31] She was unable to find witnesses to back up the recruitment story and residents of Cheju, including a local historian who looked into the matter for several years, shrugged it off as "fabrication."[32] As people began to seriously question the validity of Yoshida's 'confessional' stories, Professor Yoshiaki Yoshimi, Japan's leading proponent of its wartime culpability issues, concluded that he could not utilize those accounts as evidence against Japan's comfort women system.[33] Unfortunately, with major newspapers such as

---

26 Ibid., p.237.

27 Ibid.

28 Ibid., p.230.

29 Ibid., p.237.

30 Ibid.

31 Soh, p.153.

32 Ibid.

33 Hata, p.242.

Asahi publishing Yoshida's fraudulent accounts repeatedly, many scholars and activists relied on them to corroborate the notion of Japan's forcible recruitment of women for sexual slavery, not the least of which by Special Rapporteur Radhika Coomaraswamy for her 1996 U.N. report.[34]

On August 14, 2014, almost 32 years after its first story on Yoshida's now widely discredited stories had been published, *Asahi Shimbun* retracted all previous articles on the matter[35], admitting that after further investigation, "a number of contradictions regarding the core elements" of his accounts became undeniable.[36] In a predictable fashion, however, *Asahi* maintained that at the time the articles were published, it was "unable to uncover the falseness" of Yoshida's stories.[37]

In recent years, more official documents during World War II have been unveiled, including an archived U.S. military report entitled "Composite Report on Three Korean Navy Civilians, List No. 78, Dated 28 Mar 1945, RE "Special Questions on Koreans." This military report

---

34 Yoshimi wrote a letter to U.N. Special Rapporteur Coomaraswamy advising her to delete texts related to Yoshida's claims from her 1996 report on comfort women. Hata, p.280.

35 Yoshida, R. (August 5, 2014) Asahi Shimbun admits errors in past 'comfort women' stories. *The Japan Times*. (https://www.japantimes.co.jp/news/2014/08/05/national/politics-diplomacy/asahi-shimbun-admits-errors-in-past-comfort-women-stories/#.WpSQCExFzIV)

36 Testimony about 'forcible taking away of women on Jeju Island': Judged to be fabrication because supporting evidence not found. (August 22, 2014) *Asahi Shimbun Digital*. (https://www.asahi.com/articles/SDI201408213563.html)

37 Asahi's explanation reads, "We were unable to uncover the falseness of his testimony at the time the articles were published."

written by American soldiers who conducted interrogations of three captured Korean civilians of the Japanese Navy offers a genuine mindset of the Korean people of that era which includes their common knowledge of the comfort women system. While the anti-Japanese sentiment among the Korean population is quite evident[38], the report summed up their understanding that "All Korean prostitutes that POW have seen in the Pacific were volunteers or had been sold by their parents into prostitution."[39]

Apart from acknowledging the realities of how women became comfort women, they categorically rejected any notion of an institutionalized, systematic abduction, forced recruitment or conscription by the Japanese military to have been possible:

> This is proper in the Korean way of thinking but direct conscription of women by the Japanese would be an outrage that the old and young alike would not tolerate. Men would rise up in a rage, killing Japanese no matter what consequences they might suffer.[40]

---

38 Item 19 reads: "Older Koreans who lived in the days of Korean independence invariably hate the Japanese. While some younger men who have attended Japanese schools are outwardly pro-Japanese; many of them are most outspoken in their feelings against the Japanese rule."

39 Report on Three Korean Navy Civilians, List No. 78, Dated 28 Mar 45, RE "Special Questions on Koreans." By Lt. Wilson, dated 24 April 1945, based on interrogation of three Korean civilians; date of interrogation: 11 April 1945. Military Intelligence Service, Captured Personnel & Material Branch, item 18. (http://cdn.mainichi.jp/vol1/2016/06/10/20160610p2a00m0na015000q/0.pdf)

40 Ibid.

MILITARY INTELLIGENCE SERVICE
CAPTURED PERSONNEL & MATERIAL BRANCH

Date of Report: 24 April 1945.
Date of Interrogation: 11 April 1945.
Serial Nos and Rank: 41J-1150, Civilian, LEE, Bok Do
14J-185, Civilian, PAIK, Song Kum
41J-393, Civilian, KANG, Ki Nam

By: Lt. Wilson

COMPOSITE REPORT ON THREE KOREAN NAVY CIVILIANS, LIST NO. 78, DATED 28 MAR 45, RE "SPECIAL QUESTIONS ON KOREANS."

1538

PREAMBLE

The general anti-Japanese feeling of these Koreans is the same as almost all of some 100 Korean PsW questioned by the interrogator. It is probable that some Koreans are opportunists but these 3 appear to be very sincere in their statements which may be considered reliable. A separate report will be made on one PW; the other two are not worth further interrogation.

QUESTIONNAIRE

This report is based on "Interrogations of Koreans", List No. 78 of 28 Mar 45. Paragraph numbers correspond to question numbers in this list.

2. **Koreans in Local Government**:

   a. The village headman is always a Korean. He is an elderly man elected by the villagers for his honesty and leadership. The Japanese make no attempt to control the election.

18. All Korean prostitutes that PsW have seen in the Pacific were volunteers or had been sold by their parents into prostitution. This is proper in the Korean way of thinking but direct conscription of women by the Japanese would be an outrage that the old and young alike would not tolerate. Men would rise up in a rage, killing Japanese no matter what consequence they might suffer.

Considering certain incidents fueled by ethnic nationalism across Korea during Japan's annexation period that involved grievances and the demand for independence[41], an utterly grotesque, criminal act of organized seizure of their daughters and wives, the paradigmatic story of forcible recruitment by the Japanese military, if true, would have certainly resulted in an insurrection all over the peninsula. One may draw a parallel with FDR's Executive Order 9066 that authorized the internment of Japanese-Americans in the Western United States shortly after Japan's bombing of Pearl Harbor. However, the unfortunate wartime measure to relocate U.S. citizens of a certain ancestry was not about sending away only female members of families, but often entire families based upon racial and ethnic targeting and discrimination; it had nothing to do with taking advantage of defenseless women to satiate the sexual needs of soldiers or other men.

Further, the executive order was just that – an executive decision by the U.S. President and Commander-in-Chief. As reviewed in previous sections, neither the recruiting of comfort women nor its specific method, as far as we can find,

---

41 As an example, what has been called the March First Movement of 1919 erupted to repudiate Japanese rule and demand Korean independence on March 1, and lasted for months, initially through nonviolent street demonstrations after proclaiming the declaration of independence. This movement, though devoid of central leadership or organization, would spread into major cities and later engage in bloody confrontations with police, civilian officials, attacks on property, and even an assassination attempt of a governor general. About 300,000 is one very rough estimate of the total number of participants. Baldwin, Frank, "Participatory Anti-Imperialism: The 1919 Independence Movement." Journal of Korean Studies, vol.1, 1979, pp.124-132, 135.

had been ordered by any Japanese military high command. Instead, the recruiting process itself seems to have been generally relied on proprietors, recruiters, and agents in the industry. Particularly in Korea, "it was rare that military personnel were directly involved in recruiting women"[42] since labor brokers and others with experience in that line of work already existed for many years. Korean natives enjoyed a linguistic advantage as many were bilingual in Japanese, in contrast to most Japanese who did not speak Korean. Therefore, by virtue of the original testimonial narratives of the women survivors, the opinion that it was mainly the agents, recruiters, and proprietors who procured the women to comfort stations[43] ought to be deemed the historical reality of the Korean comfort women experience.

---

42 Henson, xiv.

43 Park, p.101.

Conclusion

While isolated cases of 'forcible recruitment,' i.e., methods of abduction and other coercive means apparently occurred in the newly occupied territories such as the Dutch East Indies and the Philippines, these incidents in no consequential manner validate the allegation of an organized, institutionalized criminal recruiting system carried out by the Japanese military. The Philippines had comfort stations that followed written military rules and regulations including hygienic and other safety measures for the women and the soldiers when engaging in sexual contact, which obviously did not coincide with the dreadful environment where victims such as Maria Rosa Henson[44] and others endured.

With respect to the Dutch East Indies, the unfortunate illegal acts represented by the Semarang Incident involved a forcible taking of women from POW camps contrary to military policy and specific advice by a regional higher command to obtain consent from women prior to becoming comfort women. The brothels were ordered to be shut down by the command post in Jakarta, the 16th Army Headquarters, and those who committed the crimes were prosecuted and found guilty by the post-WWII Temporary War Tribunal at Batavia. For this reason, there are solid grounds to embrace Jan Ruff O'Herne's condemnation of the term comfort woman as "an insult" as well as recognizing her and others as "war

---

44 In 1996, Maria Henson received $19,000 of 'atonement money' via the Asian Women's Fund, a private organization backed by the Japanese government. Mydans, S. (August 27, 1997) Maria Rosa Henson, 69, Dies; Victim of Japanese Brothels. *New York Times*.

rape victims, enslaved and conscripted."[45] In order to resolve private claims by certain individuals, Japan compensated the Dutch government US$10 million in 1956.[46]

The situation in annexed Korea proves to be a complex and tragic experience in which certain parents had no choice but to sacrifice their daughters for economic survival, many young women who sought to better their lives being deceived by comfort women procurers, and others who simply chose to become sexual laborers out of their own volition. Although the Korean activists together with their international allies in human rights and feminist camps skillfully solidified the global paradigm of "forcible recruitment by the Japanese military," more original source documents such as World War II military records and others have come into the public arena in recent years.

Testimonial narratives of former comfort women, at least at this time, appear to be the only source the activists of the redress movement rely on to support the paradigm, devoid of substantive corroboration. The testimonials vary among the women in terms of how they were recruited, and some have clearly altered their stories to be harmonious with the paradigm. Even by focusing on the Korean Peninsula alone, the Japanese military having engaged in an organized, systematic coercive recruitment of comfort women, though highly effective in making news headlines, can only be deemed illogical and misguided given among other factors, how law enforcement responded to human traffickers and how families would have resisted to protect their women as well as their honor. Instead, in light of the material covered in the previous

---

45 Soh, pp.71-72.

46 Yoshimi, p.176.

sections, it may not have been an exaggeration for Professor Bruce Cumings to comment back in 1997 that "many of the women were mobilized by Korean men."[47] What has emerged more than anything after reviewing different territories with comfort women is a diverse range of recruiting, both legal and illegal, that cannot by any stretch be judged systematic and organized pursuant to a high military command of the Japanese Imperial Forces.

---

47 Cumings, p.178.

PART II

Sexual Slavery

A. Terminology and Types of Comfort Stations

Since the paradigmatic story also involves 'sexual slavery' as the ends to the means of 'forcible recruitment by the Japanese military,' it logically warrants a focused attention to that very term. Sexual slavery, sometimes also referred to as sexual exploitation, has been defined as attaching the right of ownership over one or more persons with the intent to coerce or force them to engage in sexual activities.[1] It obviously includes forced prostitution, and in the opinion of one feminist scholar, female sexual slavery "is present in ALL situations where women and girls cannot change the immediate conditions of their existence; where regardless of how they got into those conditions they cannot get out; and where they are subject to sexual violence and exploitation."[2] This scholar further asserts that because organizations that have conducted extensive research on the exploitation of women in prostitution found 80% to 95% of all prostitution is "pimp controlled," any prostitution that is not pimp controlled cannot be regarded as slavery, but a form of sexual exploitation.[3] In other words, the social condition "that requires escape in order for the victim to get out of it" establishes the person's status as a slave.[4]

---

1 Jones, Jacki, Frear, Anna, Fenton, Rachel Anne, and Stevenson, Kim, *Gender, Sexualities and Law*, Routledge, New York, (2011), p. 203.

2 Barry, Kathleen, *The Prostitution of Sexuality: Global Exploitation of Women*, New York University Press, New York, (1995), p. 199.

3 Ibid., pp.198-200.

4 Ibid., pp.199-200.

By definition, any form of slavery must involve a 'master' and a 'slave,' i.e., someone with complete or close to unconditional power over the servant or subordinate. In the U.S. Interrogation Report No. 49, one of the military reports presented in Part I, the comfort women identified the "house master" as the couple that had recruited and later employed the women after advancing money to their parents.[5] The very fact that the women referred to the couple as "house master" may prove to be more significant as particulars of the comfort stations are explored further.

As we have learned from Part I, comfort stations had variations insofar as the extent of military involvement, whether in terms of how women were recruited (including criminal acts) or the operation of the facility itself. Scholars have presented different ways to categorize comfort stations that reflected their specific interests. For instance, Professor Yoshimi has classified them into three types: a) comfort stations directly run by the military for its exclusive use; b) civilian-managed but supervised and regulated by the military for its exclusive use (found to be the most common); and c) other facilities such as restaurants and bars for the general public but designated as comfort stations, with the military given special priority.[6]

Another categorization consists of a) permanent (in major cities), b) semipermanent (assigned to sizable military units), and c) temporary (by small units close to the front lines), emphasizing how long the facilities were run which probably

---

5 U.S. Office of War Information, Interrogation Report No. 49, pp.1-2.

6 Soh, p.117.

depended and was also determined by the circumstances of the locales.⁷

In her classification of comfort stations, Professor Soh stresses what she calls the organizational motive of the military as opposed to the "motives behind the running, supporting, and/or patronizing" the comfort stations.⁸ By specifically highlighting the motives behind the organizing of various comfort stations, she contends that her approach serves to "better explain the nature of the comfort system."⁹

Based on "different operational factors" of the comfort stations, Soh proposes three main categories:

> a) concessionary – commercial facilities of assignation and prostitution run by civilian concessionaries for profit; the civilians (proprietors and comfort station operators) are contractually regulated by the military that sanctions the operation; the two subgroups within this category differed in that the more comprehensive facility catered to officers, offering food, alcohol, and other forms of entertainment such as dancing and singing by women; other facilities were for the rank and file without additional recreation activities; Soh's research identifies the latter type to have been where the majority of the Korean women labored;¹⁰

---

7 Ibid.

8 Ibid.

9 Ibid.

10 Ibid., pp.117-123.

b) paramilitary - run by the military as a not-for-profit comfort station and were generally located in remote front-line areas; the women were either "kept within the military compound" that included manual labor (such as nursing) or outside the compound where such labor was not usually performed;[11]

c) criminal – operated by soldiers in the battlefield that involved illegal acts of abduction, rape, and/or coercive procurement leading to confinement and sexual enslavement; in essence, "soldiers gratified their sexual needs at will and for free"; Soh argues that it was primarily during the final years of the war when this type of criminal *ianjo* (comfort station) came about, with Maria Henson being its typical confined victim.[12]

With such varying degrees of geographical, financial, and operational differences among comfort stations, it unquestionably makes a broad statement such as once there, the women "lived in a state of perpetual coercion characterized by continual rape, confinement, and physical abuse"[13] extremely challenging to substantiate, unless the characterization was specifically meant to address criminal behavior by the military.

While the categorization above illuminates an interesting aspect among the comfort stations such as being a profit-seeking enterprise or not, it may be worthwhile to also add

---

11 Ibid., pp.118-124.

12 Ibid.

13 Yoshimi, p.11.

a fourth group that Professor Yoshimi identified, i.e., other facilities including restaurants and bars for the general public but designated as brothels the Japanese military permitted the men to visit. Quite a few restaurant owners in China and Korea opted to capitalize on the military demand for sexual services across the Pacific.[14] Even the "house master" that ran the comfort station in Burma interrogated by military officers for the U.S. Interrogation Report No. 49 had been in the restaurant business in Keijo, Korea before choosing a different enterprise.[15]

Additionally, it may make sense to include brothels not designated by the military for use, since certain soldiers such as in Manila knew not to visit them, but still did (refer to Part I, Section A. Complexity in the Battleground: The Philippines). Other brothels all over the Pacific not sanctioned by the Japanese existed, and soldiers may have visited some of them. Indeed, this subgroup can logically be part of the spectrum of comfort stations, for the third type, the 'criminal comfort station,' did not operate under or even maintain a set of rules and regulations as the other two main groups of *ianjo*. Hence, brothels outside the purview of Japan's military may be included as non-military sanctioned comfort stations as long as soldiers patronized them.

---

14 Hata, p.109.

15 ATIS Research Report No. 120, p.17.

B. Purpose of Implementing a Comfort Women System

What must be clarified at this point is the *raison d'etre* of the comfort women system: the intended purpose of establishing a military brothel system by the Japanese Imperial Forces has been generally recognized, though usually concluded as quite ineffectual, to 1) regulate military sexuality and discourage battlefield sex crimes[1]; 2) prevent sexually transmitted diseases among soldiers[2]; 3) provide "comfort" to the troops[3]; and 4) protect military personnel from spies.[4]

While it has already been shown in Part I the limitations to "discourage battlefield sex crimes," certain Japanese military documents nevertheless convey such intent as one of the key reasons for having comfort stations. In a report forwarded to each army unit by the Ministry of War on September 19, 1940, it emphasized the importance of regulating "military sexuality" in order to prevent criminal acts by the soldiers.[5]

After referring to an investigation that confirmed criminal acts taken by certain soldiers "frequently occurred immediately after combat," the report recommends giving the following:

> ... careful consideration to the setting up of comfort facilities, and attend to restraining and

---

1 Soh, p.142.

2 Yoshimi, p.72.

3 Ibid.

4 Ibid.

5 Ibid., p.60.

pacifying savage feelings and lust.... The emotional effects of sexual comfort stations on soldiers should be considered the most critical. It must be understood that the competence or lack thereof in overseeing {the operation of comfort stations} has the greatest influence on the promotion of morale, the maintenance of military discipline, and the prevention of crimes and sexually transmitted diseases.[6]

In effect, the Military of War firmly believed that comfort stations served as a system to prevent crimes against the local populace in occupied enemy territories by way of raising the morale of the troops and maintaining military discipline.[7] In order to boost morale and preserve discipline among the soldiers, seeking 'comfort' with the opposite sex where combat did not erupt seems to have been the only escape for any type of human contact, easing physical and psychological wounds even for a brief period.

While there have been disagreements as to where the first comfort station was established (the consensus is somewhere in China in early 1930s - more on this topic in Part III), one of the reasons for setting up such facility dealt with the military's policy to protect soldiers from contracting venereal diseases.[8] As the standard rule, the Japanese military did not permit troops to use civilian brothels in enemy territories.

In order to prevent the spread of sexually transmitted diseases and espionage, comfort station operators were

---

[6] Ibid. Text from Summary of "Measures to Enhance Military Discipline in Light of the Experiences of the China Incident," dated September 19, 1940 by Japan's Ministry of War.

[7] Ibid.

[8] Ibid., p.47.

required to "submit daily reports on the number of soldiers serviced, the amount of money earned, and the number of condoms used by each comfort woman."[9]

Being a system designed by and for the military, the comfort stations only allowed non-military visitors pursuant to strict guidelines. Furthermore, soldiers were reminded of taking the issue of information leaks seriously when entering the comfort stations. As an example, the "Regulations for the Use of the Soldiers' Club" for a garrison stationed in Zhongshan, Guangdong Province, China, stipulate both points:

> CLAUSE NO. 17 – The use of Soldiers' Club No. 2 is restricted to military personnel and civilian employees of the army. If accompanied by an officer, however, local people [civilians] are permitted to use Soldiers' Club No. 1.[10]

> CLAUSE NO. 18 – Those visiting the clubs should be on their guard to prevent leaks of secret information [espionage prevention].[11]

China remained Japan's military adversary throughout the Pacific War which finally ended after the latter's unconditional surrender to the Allied Forces in August of 1945, and the largest number of comfort stations existed

---

9   Ibid., p.138.

10 Ibid., p.137.

11 Ibid., p.136.

there among all occupied enemy territories.[12] The following section introduces a prototype representing a large-scale facility in Central China.

---

12 Of the 400 identified comfort stations throughout Asia, 280 were located in China as of Sept. 1942. Refer to Yoshimi's *Comfort Women: Sexual Slavery in the Japanese Military During World War II*, p.86.

C. Comfort Station in Hankow, China

The city of Hankow (or Hankou), a major metropolitan area in Central China, was widely acknowledged as having the largest comfort station for the Japanese military.[1] Comprised of 68 two-story buildings, this comfort station strictly for military use located at the center of Hankow that would house 300 women opened in November 1938, and along with Wuchung (or Wuchang), a nearby city, soldiers passing through patronized it in addition to the garrisons until the end of World War II.[2]

Through numerous memoirs by soldiers and other documents and records, no other comfort station with so much available information has been identified.[3] As to which category this *ianjo* falls into, Professor Soh explains that concessionary types "were usually located in clusters, both in big cities and in isolated areas where the military units were stationed."[4] Besides being clustered with many two-storied structures in a major city, other elements such as military supervision and civilian operation of the facility will become evident in the subsequent details.

Under the supervision of Japan's 11th Army, more specifically its line of communications (supply train) headquarters, the comfort women were either Japanese or Korean, but there appears to have been brothels outside the

---

1 Hata, p.90.

2 Ibid.

3 Ibid.

4 Soh, p.123.

jurisdiction of the Japanese military with local Chinese women in surrounding areas.[5]

Aside from precluding the risk of espionage by the native women of China, even the Poelgeest Report acknowledged the other reason for transporting Japanese and Korean women to China to labor as comfort women:

> During the war in China in the 1930s, the occurrence of venereal disease among the troops had led to problems with deployment and the Japanese military forces therefore decided to set up military brothels as a preventive measure. In addition to local women, Japanese and Korean women - Korea being part of the Japanese Empire – were recruited for the brothels in China.[6]

According to a Hankow military organizational chart dated 1943, the line of communications headquarters of Japan's 11th Army oversaw many departments including those dealing with the affairs of restaurants, cafeterias, lodging facilities, theatres, amusement areas, libraries, POW camps, military doctors, and **comfort women**.[7] Since much of the previous material in Part I delved into the recruiting process of comfort women, the series of steps once the women arrived at comfort stations serves as a good starting point to study various aspects of comfort stations.

Members of the department in charge of comfort women matters first undertook the registration of the women after

---

5 Hata, pp.90-91.

6 Poelgeest Translation, p.3.

7 Hata, p.92.

they arrived. An outline of the registration procedure is given below:

> 1. A noncommissioned officer examined the comfort woman's photograph, a copy of her family registry, her written pledge, her parental consent form, her permit from police, her identification papers from local officials where she lived, and similar documents.
>
> 2. Then he filled out a prescribed personal examination form, recording her personal history, her guardians' addresses and occupations, the makeup of her family, the amount of cash advanced to her or her family. This information was later supplemented with reports of such events as her departure from business or a hospitalization. Comments on her character, such as "she has a habit of drinking," were also added as time passed.
>
> 3. A copy of the personal examination form was sent to military police.[8]

As a noteworthy point about the organizational chart, it includes a union (or association) comprised of workers at the comfort station, with a Japanese being the head and an ethnic Korean as the deputy head.[9] In Part I that details the comfort stations in the Philippines, "associations" were mentioned to operate those located in Tacloban (refer to Section A.

---

8 Yoshimi, p.135.

9 Hata, p.92.

Complexity in the Battleground: The Philippines), but that does not appear to be the case in Hankow.

First Lieutenant Kiyokichi Yamada, who became section chief on comfort women matters in February 1943, focused on 1) allowing the women to be able to repay the debt so that they can return home; and 2) setting the price so that soldiers could afford visiting the comfort station.[10] With these two seemingly antithetical objectives in mind, his role to oversee the comfort station proved to be anything but an easy task. Furthermore, his work also involved taking on seasoned comfort station proprietors and operators.[11] This supervisory function by the military during wartime had a precedence – the police played this role in a time of peace as part of maintaining Japan's licensed prostitution.[12]

As stated in his memoir, when he inquired the women who arrived in Hankow whether they can endure this kind of trying labor, he found that they uniformly understood the nature of the work involved.[13] However, in the fall of 1944, when a young Korean woman who arrived as part of a group of roughly 30 recruited by two compatriots, she started weeping upon learning the type of work she had been brought to perform. Yamada quickly instructed the comfort station operator to arrange some other work for her.[14] Kenichi Nagasawa, fellow First Lieutenant and military doctor for the

---

10 Ibid., p.91.

11 Ibid.

12 Ibid., p.270.

13 Ibid., p.93.

14 Ibid.

comfort station, commented that most likely some smooth-talking recruiter tricked her into coming along.[15]

Other scholars have noted the Japanese military's handling of such situations. In one instance, after several young women complained to the officers that they had no idea why they were brought to a comfort station by recruiters, their return to Korea was arranged.[16] In another case that dealt with a woman becoming ill, her discharge was arranged by an officer, allowing her to return home.[17]

What Lieutenant Yamada advised all the comfort women as soon as he took charge was not to waste money or live in luxury, but to pay debts and return home so that they could live a happy family life.[18] While he personally felt they could repay debts in about eighteen months and possibly enjoy some savings by working beyond that period[19], here are a few examples of how the women fared:

> A woman who labored under the name of Haruko sent money back to her parents in Korea to buy back crop fields they had lost;[20]
> Another woman, Keiko, planned to save 30,000 to 50,000 yen in order to start a small restaurant in Keijo (present-day Seoul). This impressed a

---

15 Ibid.

16 Park, p.97.

17 Ibid., p.95.

18 Hata, p.392.

19 Ibid.

20 Ibid.

commander so much that he considered issuing a letter of commendation to her;[21]

Hankow being a city with the largest comfort station in China, the women certainly participated in athletic and theatrical events[22] which corresponds with the activities mentioned in the U.S. Interrogation Report No. 49: "... they amused themselves by participating in sports events with both officers and men, and attended picnics, entertainments, and social dinners.[23]

In his published account on his years at Hankow, Nagasawa, the military doctor, states that almost all of the women managed to repay their debts and later became part of the community, by helping men who were discharged by the army run a business or working at bars and other establishments.[24]

Identical to the pricings at other comfort stations, a three-tiered system existed in Hankow: 1.00 yen for enlisted soldiers; 1.50 yen for non-commissioned officers; and 3.00 yen for officers. The women's percentage ranged between 40% and 50% while their monthly incomes fluctuated from 400 to 500 yen.[25] This income range does not deviate much from the figures given by the U.S. Interrogation Report No.

---

21 Ibid.

22 Ibid., p.393.

23 U.S. Office of War Information, Interrogation Report No. 49, p.2.

24 Nagasawa, Kenichi, *Kankō Ianjo* (Hankow Comfort Station), Tosho Shuppan, Tokyo, (1983) p.227. His book notes the number of proprietors at 30 for 300 women. Ibid., p.56.

25 Hata, p.389.

49, with the women's average monthly income being 750 yen after half of the gross went to the "house master."[26]

The pricing commonly set for the enlisted soldiers at different comfort stations throughout Asia, from parts of China to Burma to the Philippines seems to have been between 1.00 and 1.50 yen.[27] Even so, considering the monthly pay of an enlisted soldier from 6 to 10 yen, going to a comfort station often could not have been financially possible even if allowed. The Australian POW Gordon Thomas remarked that "Each man was entitled to a permit to visit once every two weeks," which probably reflected the military's consideration, among other factors, the soldiers' ability to pay given their income. What becomes intriguing is that, if the comfort women earned anywhere near as what these sources reveal, then they were placed in a financially profitable position unparalleled by the vast majority of military men who had to give up a good fraction of their monthly pay for a brief encounter.[28]

---

26 U.S. Office of War Information, Interrogation Report No. 49, p.3.

27 Hata, p.389. Pricings at different locales are given.

28 Former comfort women have stated in their testimonials that "most left after about five minutes of sexual contact," even though the standard time was for 30 minutes. Soh, p.123. In a similar fashion, once the U.S. declared war against Japan on Dec. 8, 1941, servicemen in Hawaii "paid three dollars for three minutes of the only intimacy most were going to find in Honolulu." Bailey, Beth and Farber, David, *The First Strange Place*, Johns Hopkins University Press, Baltimore, (1994), p.95.

D. Details from a Comfort Station Manager's Diary

One of the new discoveries in recent years on Japan's comfort women system concerns a diary written by a person who managed facilities in Burma and Singapore. Purchased at a used bookstore by a curator of a museum in Paju, South Korea, this diary quickly caught the attention of scholars including Ahn Byung-jik, Professor Emeritus of Seoul National University, who translated the text into modern Korean. The diary by Mr. Bak (or Park) covered 36 years of his life including the experience at comfort stations from January 1, 1943 to December 31, 1944, a period of two years, and an English translation of entries during that period along with commentaries by Professor Choe Kil-sung can be accessed online.[1]

Working at the front desk of a comfort station from 2pm to about 1am, the author of the diary recorded the daily earnings in his ledger and performed the followings as part of his function:

> He rose early each morning and after breakfast he went shopping in the marketplace with his page. Upon his return, his duties included drawing up statements of income and expenditure, attending regular meetings, adjusting accounts, going on air raid watches at the office of the club association, managing the savings of the comfort women, distributing rations, participating

---

[1] Diary of a Japanese Military Brothel Manager, Chapter 5, English Translation (hereinafter "Diary Translation": http://www.sdh-fact.com/CL/Chapter-51.pdf)

in the Civil Defense Corps and celebratory events, procuring entry permits at the Military Administration Headquarters, remitting money to the field post office, Hua Nan Bank, Yokohama Specie Bank, and the Southern Development Bank, submitting the employment permits of comfort women, having his car checked, paying workmen, rationing rice, etc...[2]

His personal life seemed quite luxurious than most military men and civilians at the time, purchasing "nine yards of Western fabrics for seventy yen" and various clothes such as "clothing worth over 350 yen from a wool clothing store," in addition to owning a car and even considering acquiring a wristwatch at 750 yen.[3] However, the diary makes it clear that he was not part of the Japanese military, and he was treated differently from its civilian employees as well:

> I went to have dinner at Kikusui Restaurant with Oishi, Toyokawa, Mita, Oyama, and the gang, but I was told that only soldiers and civilian military employees were allowed to enter, so we stepped out onto China Street instead and had dinner there.[4]

In January of 1944, the penultimate year of WWII, the cordial relationship he enjoyed with the military civilians began to change:

---

[2] Diary Translation, p.6.
[3] Ibid., pp.6-7.
[4] Ibid., p.7.

Inconvenient and Uncomfortable 103

> I went out to eat with army-affiliated civilians, but, starting from tomorrow, I won't be able to eat there anymore.[5]

A series of entries made in 1943 pertains to comfort stations in Mandalay and Arakan having to relocate as part of the military's logistical decisions.[6] Interestingly, the comfort women working for a fellow proprietor/manager Mr. Kanagawa (identified as ethnic Korean)[7] refusing to relocate after being told of the decision is noted:

> He ordered them to move, but I heard that the comfort women were all resolutely opposed to it and would not go.[8]

Some days later, the matter was resolved as the military commanded absolute authority within its jurisdiction:

> Ultimately, they couldn't overrule an order from the headquarters. The comfort station was moved to Yeu.[9]

Yet, the mere fact that the women expressing their objection to a relocation pursuant to a military order manifests a certain level of latitude given to the women instead of being reduced to a miserable slavelike existence without any say

---

5 Ibid.
6 Ibid., p.9.
7 Ibid., p.10.
8 Ibid., p.9.
9 Ibid.

whatsoever. According to Australian POW Gordon Thomas, the freezer he managed being the food supply for the troops in Rabaul, "the Little Ladies from the brothels swarmed around the place on every opportunity" and sometimes "they would completely take charge of the place," using his cooking utensils, crockery, a gramophone to play music, and even sleeping on his bed.[10]

By September of 1943, Mr. Bak was on his way to Singapore, the new locale for a comfort station he would manage until the end of 1944.[11] Not being a member of the military, "standard means of transportation" such as trains, boats, cars, and carriages allowed him to reach his destination, although he wrote about hitching a ride on a military train when regular trains were not operating.[12]

The diary goes on to describe the manager's function to obtain permits for the comfort women (referred as "barmaid" and "workwoman" below) to work as well as dealing with their health issues:

> I got a permit for the barmaid.[13]
>
> I received a medical certificate for the barmaid...[14]
>
> I went to the official in charge of business at the Peace Preservation Section of the Singapore Police

---

10 Thomas, p.85.

11 Diary Translation, pp.10-11.

12 Ibid., p.10.

13 Ibid., p.13.

14 Ibid.

Department and applied for employment permits for the workwomen.[15]

I undertook the necessary procedures for her and made her a workwoman at the clubhouse.[16]

I went to the official in charge of business at the Peace Preservation Section and had him issue the necessary certificate to apply for travel papers for a comfort woman at my clubhouse...[17]

... a comfort woman from Sakura Club, was suffering from considerable abdominal pain and in the afternoon I was told that she underwent surgery. During her seventh month of pregnancy there were abnormalities with the way the baby was kicking. She was admitted to Suzuki Hospital, but miscarried and was driven back here.[18]

The comfort workwoman Tamae is currently seven-months pregnant and so I gave her a leave of absence from work.[19]

Although the timing of the leave of absence given to the woman proves troublesome, the diary includes instances of women leaving comfort stations:

---

15 Ibid., p.14.
16 Ibid.
17 Ibid., p.17.
18 Ibid., p.14.
19 Ibid.

> Two comfort women, Junko and Osome, quit their jobs.[20]

> Haruyo and Hiroko had worked at Mr. Murayama's comfort station, but they left in order to live with their husbands. Logistics ordered them to return and now they are working as comfort women at Kinsen House.[21]

The diary does not state the reason for the military to order the return of the women, but certain others appear to have left without any issue. Hence, once again, these entries portray the women to have enjoyed a certain degree of movement and the freedom to go back to their homeland, provided that the military considered the return journey to be safe (and debts have been settled). The U.S. Interrogation Report No. 49 contains a comment on women returning home from Burma: "In the latter part of 1943 the Army issued orders that certain girls who had paid their debt could return home. Some of the girls were thus allowed to return to Korea."[22]

Medical checkups of the women and the inspection of the comfort station being conducted are conveyed as well:

> The army doctors from logistics inspected the comfort women even for syphilis.[23]

---

20 Ibid.

21 Ibid.

22 U.S. Office of War Information, Interrogation Report No. 49, p.3.

23 Diary Translation, p.16.

> I went to the clinic for comfort women and had a couple of unregistered comfort women examined.[24]
>
> Mr. Sakaguchi, who is in charge of business at the municipal Peace Preservation Section, and Dr. Yoshioka of Nadeshiko Hospital stopped by at around 10:00 PM and inspected the business and its washing facilities.[25]

Other entries in the diary disclose his additional function as depositing savings of the comfort women at banks as well as arranging remittance on behalf of them:

> I went to the Specie Bank and deposited the savings of two comfort women working at Mr. Maruyama's comfort station.[26]
>
> I deposited money for the workwomen.[27]
>
> I deposited 32,000 yen at the Rangoon branch of Yokohama Specie Bank.[28]
>
> At the request of a comfort woman, I withdrew six hundred yen from her savings for remittance and then sent it out via the Central Post Office.[29]

---

24 Ibid.

25 Ibid.

26 Ibid., p.14.

27 Ibid.

28 Ibid., p.15.

29 Ibid.

Being the manager of a comfort station, Mr. Bak had meetings with colleagues from other locales and paid association fees:

> I paid a total of 62 yen in dues to the Comfort Station Association, including thirty yen for myself and two yen for each of my sixteen comfort women.[30]

> There was a meeting of comfort station managers at my headquarters.[31]

Of the many functions he performed as the manager of a comfort station, submitting reports of the business remained one of the most crucial:

> I presented my clubhouse's monthly report for the end of the month of August to the office of the association.[32]

> I submitted a daily business report to the logistics headquarters and received condoms.[33]

Supplying condoms by the military appears to have been part of the general routine, and likewise, their utilization by soldiers was effected through the enforcement of guidelines established for the comfort stations:

---

30 Ibid.
31 Ibid., p.18.
32 Ibid.
33 Ibid.

6. Hostesses will refuse pleasure to those who do not use prophylactic rubbers.[34]

In terms of the comfort women's safety, the *Kempeitai*, Japan's military police, monitored the premises to prevent potential trouble with the soldiers, and this entry may have been an example of 'unwanted advances' by someone from the military:

> The military employee came to the clubhouse to see the barmaid Kikue, but was discovered by the military police.[35]

The *Kempeitai* had a duty to protect civilians from violence, even insults if they were directed at comfort women.[36] The comfort women were not members of the military and looked upon as civilians. This point will be discussed further in a later section.

---

34 ATIS Research Report No. 120, p.17.

35 Diary Translation, p.14.

36 Park, p.94.

E. Comfort Station as a Business Enterprise

The previous passages in the diary exhibit informative accounts of how a comfort station manager went about his affairs, from completing business reports, attending comfort station association meetings, to even making deposits and transfer of funds at the behest of the comfort women. The entries also authenticate many of the regulations enumerated in prior sections such as obtaining a permit for the women to work, performing medical checkups, and submitting daily reports to military authorities.

Nevertheless, the entries dealing with the business aspects of the comfort station probably divulge Mr. Bak's honest feelings more than the rest, including how he describes the women when business is slow:

> We have had fewer customers than ever before since January 2. We managed to sell only fourteen tickets to soldiers.[1]

> Our customer traffic has hit rock bottom recently. We aren't able to do any business. Because we are all just spending our time idly, the comfort women are also terribly bored.[2]

After moving to Singapore, he wrote about his most profitable day yet in an entry dated April 29, 1944:

---

1 Diary Translation, p.15.

2 Ibid.

Inconvenient and Uncomfortable 111

> Today, being a holiday on account of the Emperor's birthday, we were visited by many soldiers and the club had its best day since we set up shop, raking in over 2,450 yen in revenue.[3]

Regardless, what one must bear in mind is the ever-changing surrounding environment by the war and other variables that definitely affected the business:

> An Indian man got the plague and now three to four cases have been reported. The soldiers are not allowed to go out.[4]

> The military police came and said that we were to cease operations for one week and would not be allowed to go out.[5]

As the year of 1944 was drawing to a close, Mr. Bak decided to resign as a comfort station manager, and he began taking procedural steps to do so:

> I submitted a notice of termination of employment for my job at the front desk of Kikusui with the official in charge of business at the Peace Preservation Section.[6]

---

3 Ibid., p.16.
4 Ibid.
5 Ibid.
6 Ibid., p.17.

> I submitted an application for travel papers so that Hidemi can return home.[7]

> I submitted an application for travel papers for the waitress Lee... with the official in charge of travel papers.[8]

Without question, these entries demonstrate the legitimate business nature of the comfort station, with the purpose of maximizing profit inasmuch as the situation allowed given the ongoing war in the Pacific. In like manner, the comfort women needed to transact business to earn, and not having clients for whatever reason resulted in no income. When Mr. Bak chose to retire from the business, requesting travel papers for those who desired to return home seemed to have been arranged.

Professor Choe Kil-sung's own commentary includes his viewpoint on the relationship between the Japanese military and the comfort stations:

> Even though the comfort women business was not a part of the military, it did have a tight connection with the military. Perhaps, upon reflection, it would be fair to say that the military and the comfort stations were in a 'special relationship.' Alternatively, one might say that the comfort stations were governed by the military administration of the territories occupied by the Japanese Army.[9]

---

7 Ibid.

8 Ibid.

9 Miyamoto, p.46.

Inconvenient and Uncomfortable 113

Notwithstanding, Professor Choe concludes that, as apparent from the previous entries, the writer of the diary Mr. Bak most certainly perceived himself as an entrepreneur and not a member of the military:

> *One might ask what kind of position Mr. Bak must have held to be living this kind of life, and yet it appears that he was just the manager of a comfort station, organizing and administering things at the front desk, and not a soldier or a civilian employee of the Japanese Army.* **Indeed, he seemed wary of military employees and always thought of his business as being independent from the men of the army.**[10]

Other entries touch upon the fact that other comfort stations familiar to Mr. Bak were actually residences of the people running them:

> I have been told that the Kanpachi Club, a comfort station in Arakan, Burma, was the home of Mr. Yamamoto. Ichifujiro, the comfort station run by Mr. Murayama in Insein just outside Rangoon, apparently is Mr. Murayama's home.[11]

> I was told that the Kikusui Club, located at 88 Cairnhill Road in Singapore's residential district, is the home of Mr. Nishihara.[12]

---

10 Ibid.
11 Diary Translation, p.12.
12 Ibid.

Such arrangement obviously differs, for instance, from the facility in Hankow, China, but once again it underscores the diverse nature of the comfort women system depending on the geographic location and other variables.

An important point Professor Choe makes in his commentary of the diary highlights the entrepreneurial spirit of ethnic Koreans during the annexation period:

> Now that they were subjects of the Japanese Empire, this was probably the first time that Koreans were going abroad to do business. The diary makes it clear that several Koreans had wide-ranging business contacts in places like Indonesia, Malaysia, Thailand, and East Timor, and in addition to comfort stations they operated a diverse range of businesses, including restaurants, cafeterias, rice cake shops, confectionaries, tofu dealerships, and oil refineries.[13]

To validate his assertion, Professor Choe explains that many people in Mr. Bak's entries were ethnic Koreans:

> ... although the diary mentions many people bearing Japanese-style names, in most cases these were Japanese-style names taken by ethnic Koreans.[14]

Mr. Bak himself wrote about his other business dealings while he was the comfort station manager:

---

[13] Miyamoto, p.47.

[14] Diary Translation, p.8. Having Korean as a native tongue, Korean proprietors appeared to recruit and employ female compatriots while Japanese counterparts hired women from Japan proper. Refer to Miyamoto, pp.37-39.

As of today I have struck a deal to jointly manage a cafeteria and an oil refinery with Mr. Oyama, and I have decided to move forward with prepping the enterprise.[15]

With such background information of many operating comfort stations as an extension of their entrepreneurial endeavors, the notion of these facilities engaging in sexual slavery, if such argument is to be substantiated, must then necessitate attention to the master-slave relationship. In the case with Mr. Bak, by reason of exercising managerial authority at the comfort station that included access to the women's earnings and health, he would be similar to the "house master" identified in the U.S. Interrogation Report No. 49 who ran the facility in Burma. Being the businessman, he dealt with military personnel who came to the comfort station as customers and the women as the laborers who needed medical checkups and other necessities.

Whether or not the comfort women system resembled any form of slavery may become clearer through prudent evaluation of a book on the experience of a former comfort woman, Mun Ok-chu.

---

15 Ibid., p.13.

F. Former Comfort Woman Mun Ok-chu

Mun Ok-chu, a former Korean comfort woman who spent three years laboring at a comfort station in Burma, was a co-plaintiff of Kim Hak-sun in the class-action lawsuit filed before the Tokyo District Court in Japan back in 1991. Known for her "proficiency in Japanese, her musical talent, and her outgoing personality"[1] that allowed her to save an enormous amount of money, her story as a popular comfort woman among the military personnel became a source for a book by a female writer in Japan.[2] Published in 1996, *Mun Oku-Chu: Biruma Sensen Tateshidan no "Ianfu" Datta Watashi* (I was a Comfort Woman of the Shield Division on the Burma Front) offers a more comprehensive account than her Korean version that came out three years earlier.[3] In this publication, Mun's vivid descriptions of her time in Burma, from Mandalay to Rangoon, and then briefly in Thailand before returning to Korea after the end of the war present invaluable insight from a first-person standpoint who dealt with the Japanese military, the comfort station manager, and also with the local populace.

While the book mainly focuses on her days at a comfort station from 1942, Mun also discloses her earlier past of having been a victim of forcible recruitment by "a man in a Japanese uniform" and taken to Manchuria in 1940.[4] Thus, her accounts in the book predominantly involve her time

---

1 Soh, p.183.

2 Ibid.

3 Ibid.

4 Ibid.

in Burma after returning to Korea (through the help of a military officer who arranged a special travel permit for her) and performing odd jobs before meeting a man in Pusan, Korea. This man, a Mr. Matsumoto, a compatriot with a Japanese surname, cajoled her to come work at a restaurant but was in fact a comfort station proprietor in Burma.[5]

Mun expresses sympathy and understanding for the soldiers who left their families in Japan, giving them solace as much as she could as they reminisced about their wives and children.[6] She makes it crystal clear that because she worked hard, she would later be invited to attend the officers' banquets to perform (sing and dance), but not all comfort women were given such opportunity. According to Mun, certain women couldn't pick up Japanese and others had trouble getting accustomed to the life in a comfort station.[7] These women would not say a word to the soldiers or be defiant, causing the men to feel uneasy and ending up in confrontations, sometimes turning physical. It appears that these types of women were the ones who always got into trouble with the soldiers.[8]

As officers found her to be a sweet and likeable character, she would receive tips from them, but she commiserated with the young men going to the front lines as being the most unfortunate, the soldiers who were the same age as she and her

---

5 Ibid.

6 Morikawa, Machiko, *Mun Oku-Chu: Biruma Sensen Tateshidan no "Ianfu" Datta Watashi*, (I was a Comfort Woman of the Shield Division on the Burma Front), Nashinoki-sha, Tokyo, (1996), p.63.

7 Ibid., p.64.

8 Ibid.

women colleagues.⁹ She believed that to them, visiting the comfort station was the only time for any kind of enjoyment, a diversion from their military duties, and for most of them, visiting the comfort station was all they would think about while on duty. Mun found the majority of the soldiers to be good-natured and honest.¹⁰

Of the many fascinating aspects of Mun the book imparts, her encouraging fellow Korean soldiers to return safely to their mutual motherland and admitting to have fallen in love as a young woman working at a comfort station invite the reader to explore a much different dimension in the comfort women issue. For one, the Korean Peninsula being an annexed territory of Japan from 1910, not only did comfort women of Korean ancestry exist, but also soldiers and officers of the same ethnicity as part of the Imperial Japanese Forces.¹¹ Korean soldiers fought valiantly for Imperial Japan and they too visited comfort stations.¹² Many officers and over half a dozen generals in the Imperial Forces were ethnic Koreans.¹³ Had Korean comfort women constituted a large percentage of the entire comfort women work force, they inevitably must have dealt with compatriot soldiers from the peninsula more often than not.

---

9 Ibid., p.65.

10 Ibid.

11 According to Japan's 1990 Ministry of Health and Welfare statistics report, over 242,000 Korean and 207,000 Taiwanese men served in the Imperial Forces during the Pacific War.

12 Park, p.173. Comfort women also dealt with Taiwanese soldiers and Indonesian paramilitary auxiliaries for the Japanese military. Soh, p.193.

13 Miyamoto, p.8.

Inconvenient and Uncomfortable 119

The man the young Mun chose as her sweetheart not only was Japanese, but an enlisted soldier who did not have any rank or power. He found her weeping outside the comfort station looking at the moon, and he inquired, "What's the matter?"[14] When she replied, "I want to see my mother in Korea," Ichirō Yamada consoled her, saying it must be tough coming to a place like this, and told her he must go to the front lines tomorrow and may not come back. Yet, he accepted it as fate being Japanese and consoled her: "You're Korean, you don't need to die. Do your best to survive and go home so that you can take good care of your parents."[15] They wept together, and this was the beginning of their brief relationship.

A few months later, Yamada returned safely from the battlefield, and Mun provides details of a major banquet welcoming him back at the comfort station. The manager Matsumoto took steps to officially close the facility for ordinary business to celebrate his return, and the comfort women contributed 1 yen each.[16] Yamada would then, according to Mun, come see her "every week," and Mun describes his visits as what she lived for, giving her a purpose in life, enabling her to endure the days at the comfort station.[17]

By contrast, Mun also mentions about how she dealt with the nasty soldiers, including those who didn't want to wear condoms, but in such case she always threatened to report

---

14 Morikawa, p.68.

15 Ibid.

16 Ibid., pp.68-69.

17 Ibid., p.74.

them to the military police or kick them hard in the groin.[18] Soldiers who have been ordered to go to the front lines were very difficult to deal with, being worked up and having the tendency to take it out on others. As for health exams for the women, she refers to weekly medical checkups undertaken by the military doctor and a combat medic.[19]

In a revealing note about the manager Matsumoto, Mun would be the leader among the women to go on strike and demand payment when he refused to pay them.[20] Once she accumulated a fair amount of cash, Mun decided to open a savings account with the aid of a soldier in the administration department, and she managed to deposit 500 yen.[21] All the soldiers held an account at the field post office, and it was her very first time having any kind of savings account.[22] For Mun who did not grow up financially well-off, it seemed like a dream as 1,000 yen would buy a small house in her hometown of Daegu (or Taegu), which would make her mother's life quite comfortable. Having such amount in the savings account gave her great pleasure, and the savings passbook became her valued treasure.[23]

In the subsequent chapters, Mun's whereabouts changes from Mandalay to Rangoon and later Thailand, then back to Rangoon before departing to Korea. Her detailed accounts often involve shopping with the women colleagues such as fruits, clothes, an alligator handbag, and a diamond. She

---

18 Ibid., p.67.

19 Ibid., p.66.

20 Ibid., p.75.

21 Ibid., pp.75-76.

22 Ibid., p.76.

23 Ibid.

even mentions attending a *kabuki* play in Rangoon performed by actors from Japan proper.[24] Because her sweetheart Yamada perished in battle, she admits that saving money as much as she could in hopes of purchasing a large house and starting a business after returning to Korea are what she now lives for.[25]

Although obtaining a travel permit that allowed her to leave Burma for Korea[26], Mun abruptly decided not to board the ship from Saigon, Vietnam, and instead rejoined the comfort station in Rangoon. She attributes her sudden change of mind to some supernatural warning not to get on the ship to Korea[27], but in either case, she did not return home until after World War II was brought to a close.[28]

But perhaps the most incredible episode in Mun Ok-chu's life as a comfort woman may be the story of her being found not guilty for killing an officer. Even though many who counterargue the redress movement allude to the amazing amount she saved in less than three years (26,145 yen in 31 months)[29], the episode of her eventual acquittal by the military court for killing a non-commissioned officer[30] truly speaks volumes about the lives of the comfort women having been anything but monolithic and simplistic.

The officer Mun claims to have stabbed in self-defense is described as being intoxicated and drawing a sword after a

---

24 Ibid., p.107.

25 Ibid., p.108.

26 Ibid., p.115.

27 Ibid., p.117.

28 Ibid., p.146.

29 Yoshimi, p.143.

30 Morikawa, p.126.

verbal exchange. The brief tussle ends as she tackles him, forcing him to drop the sword and then plunging it into his chest. Mun is sent to a military cell and the officer expires some days later, but her story includes a dramatic ending with soldiers rallying for her release while she is being tried at court-martial.[31] Mun states that the soldiers applauded her acquittal, and although some question her story's credibility, her continued popularity among the troops cannot be contested.

If operating a comfort station represented a business opportunity for entrepreneurs, the reality must have been to maximize profits as an enterprise, as inferred by the U.S. military in the ATIS Research Report commenting on brothels in Manila:

> Many managers are interested in nothing beyond their own profit, and do their job with no other purpose.[32]

On the other hand, women at the comfort stations worked to earn based on a pricing structure designed for them to eventually pay off their debts and possibly save some money, and while Korean women survivors state in their testimonial narratives as having never been paid for their services[33], various records including original source documents (e.g., U.S. Interrogation Report No. 49) indicate otherwise. Professor Yoshimi has emphasized the human rights

---

31 Hata, p.184.

32 ATIS Research Report, No. 120, p.33.

33 Soh, p.166. Proprietors applied the women's income towards debt settlement, and cash payments were not offered until later. Nagasawa, p.64.

violations of women[34], yet he acknowledges that "in many cases the military comfort stations did pay the women."[35] At this juncture, an impartial observer would realize that the idea of the women having been remunerated in any way poses a serious problem for the comfort women paradigm - once the comfort women redress movement was launched internationally in the early 1990s, the fact that the women had been paid for their labor quickly became "socially unacceptable and politically embarrassing" in South Korea.[36]

For some comfort women to later operate comfort stations themselves[37] can only be considered as a decision to earn a living, and most likely the work environment did not require them to engage in an authoritarian master-slave relationship. If Mun Ok-chu's love affair with the enlisted soldier proves anything, comfort stations involved innumerable human drama between the comfort women and the military men who visited them, and what the proponents of the global comfort women paradigm do not incorporate in their rhetoric will be the next topic for deliberation.

---

34 Yoshimi contends that the Japanese licensed prostitution itself was a form of sexual slavery with the comfort women system being an extension of it. Yoshimi, pp.203-205. He also argues that because Japanese military law did not protect comfort women, they were "nothing more than sex slaves." Yoshimi, p.151.

35 Yoshimi, p.206. Certain proprietors seemed to have taken advantage of the women by entering less visits by soldiers in the books, but such manipulation proved difficult for the military to catch. Nagasawa, p.64.

36 Soh, p.166.

37 Park, p.112.

G. Human Drama and Intimacy at Comfort Stations

Through the pen of a sympathetic feminist journalist, Mun Ok-chu has provided an enriching personal account filled with human elements of a life at a comfort station. Many other comfort women from the Korean Peninsula had been given Japanese names[1], and it has been interpreted that the names reflected their being part of Imperial Japan[2] as opposed to being members of (occupied) enemy territories. This fundamental difference made love affairs and marriages with Japanese soldiers possible.[3] The U.S. Interrogation Report No. 49 explicitly documents such relationships: "...there were numerous instances of proposals of marriage and in certain cases marriages actually took place."[4]

Recipients of such marriage proposals include Yi Sun-ok, Song Sin-do, and Ha Yong-i.[5] Pak Pok-sun, betrothed to a certain sergeant who taught her one-half of a song but never returned to share with her the other half, maintained her enduring love for the man and never married. Believing he killed himself after Japan's defeat, she kept singing the song for sixty years.[6] Chang Chun-wol met an officer who took her to his home in Tokyo where they stayed for about three

---

1 Soh, p.123.

2 Park, pp.77-80.

3 Ibid.

4 U.S. Office of War Information, Interrogation Report No. 49, p.4.

5 Soh, pp.181-182. Not surprisingly, such proposals or "connubial unions" between Korean women and men are also documented. Soh, 182.

6 Ibid., pp.185-186.

months, meeting his parents who ran a general store.[7] The officer and his parents treated her well with gifts and cash, allowing her to repay the debt to return to Korea. Although the plan was to be together after the war, she would never hear from the officer after he left for battle.[8]

Pae Chok-kan's relationship with one Ishikawa, another soldier who proposed to marry her after the war and kept breaking military rules to keep seeing her[9] exemplifies how comfort stations were replete with human emotion as a result of the ongoing interaction between the opposite sexes.

Kim Sun-dok who had developed a very close relationship with an officer that arranged her to return home to Korea with travel permits and money, became a source of embarrassment to the Korean activist groups in the early 1990s because she "actively solicited help from Japanese supporters" to search for the man.[10]

Even Lee Yong-su, possibly the most active among all former comfort women in the redress movement today, visited Taiwan where she labored for less than a year to perform a rite of spirit marriage in 1998 to express her love for a fallen officer in a *kamikaze* combat mission.[11] On the evening of the flight, the officer taught her a song in addition to handing Lee his photo and toiletries:

---

7   Ibid., pp.186-188.

8   Ibid., p.188.

9   Ibid., pp.189-190.

10 Ibid., p.185.

11 Ibid., p.188.

With courage I take off. Departing from Sinzhu
Golden waves and silver waves of the clouds I cross over
With no one to see me off
Toshiko alone cries for me[12]

Toshiko was the Japanese name given to her, and Lee reminisced:

> 'I'll protect you even after my death so that you may return to your ancestral land safely.' These were his last words, which I could not forget.[13]

Comfort stations being places of strong human interaction have also been affirmed by the men: a good many Japanese veterans who survived the war have recollected "nostalgically and with a certain fondness" of their experience with the women via their diaries and memoirs published prior to the genesis of the redress movement.[14] A certain veteran who has expressed sincere gratitude for the women who "comforted" the troops[15] once explained the moral code of justice and loyalty among Korean women which precluded them from dealing with men who they knew to be customers of their colleagues – no doubt this practice could be characterized as a form of 'right to refuse,' which has been noted in the U.S. Interrogation Report No. 49: "The girls were allowed the prerogative of refusing a customer."[16] To be sure, a number

---

12 Ibid.

13 Ibid., p.189.

14 Ibid., pp.190-191.

15 Ibid., p.192.

16 U.S. Office of War Information, Interrogation Report No. 49, p.3.

of Korean comfort women sometimes refer to the visiting military men as customers in their published testimonial narratives.[17] Japanese comfort women have also mentioned about not taking additional customers after getting to know a certain number of soldiers.[18]

Part of another fascinating account by the Japanese war veteran pertained to the Korean women not accepting money when they fell in love with the soldiers; the men would then bring them gifts such as special foods generally not available.[19]

Professor Park Yu-ha of South Korea believes that Korean comfort women became objects of love and affection because they were members of the Japanese Empire.[20] Soldiers gave away money to the women, cried together with them, and those who did not expect to return alive from battle gave their belongings as a parting gift.[21] In essence, the comfort women "substituted" for their hometowns and families as they bade farewell.[22]

Park maintains that soldiers came to comfort stations not only to satisfy their sexual needs, but to seek mental and psychological solace through conversation and interaction with the women. Comfort stations served a function as a place of comfort for the minds and souls of soldiers more than

---

17 Soh, p.181.

18 Hirota, Kazuko, *Shōgen Kiroku Jūgun Ianfu: Senjō ni Ikita Onna no Dōkoku* (Testimonial Records of Military Comfort Women [and] Nurses), Shinjinbutsuōraisha, Tokyo (1975), pp.72-73.

19 Soh, p.192.

20 Park, p.80.

21 Ibid., pp.80, 88.

22 Ibid., pp.85, 88.

their physical needs. In short, the *ianjo* gave relief to men who were nostalgic of their homes and to heal mental wounds from combat – they were literally 'places of comfort.'[23]

---

23 Ibid., p.85.

Conclusion

In Professor Soh's *Comfort Women*, the "private memories of genuine affection and personal compassion toward individual Japanese soldiers"[24] of numerous women mentioned earlier "provide the counternarratives" to the globally-dominant comfort women paradigm as they inject a "larger human history"[25] that indeed obfuscates and baffles it. Although Soh does not "deny the dominant images of depersonalized sexual slaves and violent rapists that have routinely been evoked,"[26] she clarifies her objective to "complicate the prevailing simplistic images by contrasting specific individual cases, which add glimpses of shared humanity between Korean comfort women and Japanese soldiers, and confounding the stereotyped portrayals of violent military hypermasculine sexuality in the dominant story."[27]

The notion of Imperial Japan's comfort women system being characterized as a form of 'sexual slavery' may only be validated if, with the term clearly defined, the living conditions in the vast majority of the comfort stations unambiguously corroborate as evidence, thereby satisfying the very definition. A sophomoric and superficial commentary that women who are "forced to render sexual services in

---

24 Soh, p.181.

25 Ibid., pp.195-196.

26 Ibid., p.181.

27 Ibid.

wartime by and/or for the use of armed forces"[28] based on careless, perfunctory conflation of wartime abduction, rape, and violence on the battlefield with highly-regulated military brothels, mostly supervised by local authorities that were still prone to horrendous mistakes (such as in Semarang), does not even begin to address the basic elements of comfort stations having been a) a business enterprise; b) that required administrative approval and operations to be supervised by local military command; and c) monitored by Japan's military police *Kempeitai* that enforced military codes.

Whereas the military commanded absolute jurisdictional authority over occupied territories, the activities within the comfort stations, although also monitored, involved proprietors and managers of the business operations exercising a mandate of all aspects of the comfort women's livelihood including pay and health issues. The comfort women spent more time with these men and their associates as they typically lived together, while soldiers and officers had to pay to spend very brief moments with them as customers. While there are two contrasting behavioral patterns of soldiers *vis-à-vis* the women ("sometimes exercising violence against them to release their tension" vs. developing "close friendly relations with non-Japanese comfort women" and treating them "with respect and compassion as fellow human beings")[29], frequent cases of love affairs and marriage proposals are documented. On the other hand, while good-natured proprietors and managers of comfort stations no doubt existed (such as Mr.

---

28 U.N. ESCOR, 52D Sess., U.N. Doc. E/CN.4 (1196), p.4. (http://www.awf.or.jp/pdf/h0004.pdf)

29 Soh, p.181.

Bak), the overall opinion of them by the women has not been positive.[30]

With the Japanese military comprised of a substantial number of ethnic Korean soldiers, if comfort stations had been places of sexual slavery involving so many of their women, more than a few violent riots and upheavals would have transpired throughout Japan's occupied territories. Instead, some former comfort women opted to enter into the business of running comfort stations. The reality is that even though some former comfort women accept the characterization of 'sex slaves' many decades later, others are certainly uncomfortable about its "degrading connotation and dislike it as well."[31]

South Korea's dominant activist group of the redress movement, Korean Council for Women Drafted for Military Sexual Slavery by Japan (often referred to by its acronym ChongDaeHyup or ChongTaeHyop), formed in November 1990, originally utilized an English name with 'Sexual Service,' not 'Sexual Slavery.'[32] Terminological history of this type definitely tells more than what is publicly espoused by their apparatchiks, but the comfort women in South Korea collectively chose not to change their official term to sex slaves when the matter was being debated in 2012. Professor Park feels that they rejected such public recognition because not only did it not convey their entire experience as comfort women accurately, it would also be an obscene attack on their pride that allowed them to endure those severe and arduous

---

30 Comfort women universally expressed hatred toward them, saying they would have killed them had there been a chance. Park, p.110.

31 Park, p.152.

32 Soh, p.72. Emphasis was added to Sexual '**Service**.'

times during the war.[33] Regardless of their true reasons, the decision not to accept the term 'sexual slavery' still stands.

---

33 Park, p.152.

PART III

The Numbers Question:
Origin of the 200,000 Claim

A. Kakō Senda

The third and final element of the prevailing narrative centers around the severity of Japan's culpability for implementing the comfort women system – that is, just how many women fell victim to the alleged organized sexual slavery? This numbers question may very well be the most symbolic of all allegations by the comfort women activists for being nebulous and often arbitrary throughout the years since the redress movement commenced. Nonetheless, it remains an integral part of the forcibly-recruited sex slave paradigm.

As a general background, comfort women had been acknowledged as part of Japan's wartime history via motion pictures (including war films), novels, and other works long before the issue became a source of diplomatic strife with South Korea that gradually morphed into an international human rights matter.

A Japanese journalist by the name of Kakō (or Kakou) Senda has been credited to bring forth comfort women as a subject matter to the general public in Japan and later South Korea with his book published in 1973.[1] Although previous publications touched upon comfort women, Senda's work focused on the women themselves, giving them a human face for the first time.[2] His 1973 book *Jūgun Ianfu* (Military Comfort Women) is comprised of his personal interviews in the early 1970s with former comfort women, war veterans, and others who had certain involvement in the military brothel

---

1 Park, p.23.

2 Ibid.

system, an era before political pressure groups invested in the issue emerged, and thus they were able to speak freely of their honest feelings about the matter. Curiously, the subtitle of the book refers to the women as "80,000 voiceless women."[3]

One of the valuable information given by Senda involves his interview with Dr. Tarō Aso whose medical report has been regarded as a key foundation for Japan's comfort women system many years later. Reflecting on the interview with Dr. Aso, Senda states that the "first comfort woman" for the Japanese military was examined by him in early spring of 1938 in Shanghai, China. While this claim is obviously an error as comfort stations existed before 1938, this book by Senda is acknowledged as a work of historical value. After making this declaration, Senda then introduces excerpts of the opinion report by Dr. Aso to the military after a series of physical examinations of 100 women who would become comfort women. In one passage, the doctor referred to the Korean comfort women as "gifts for the Emperor's Warriors"[4] or "gifts to the Imperial Armed Forces" which has been misinterpreted or misquoted by non-Japanese speaking scholars and activists as "a gift from the Emperor."[5]

---

3 Senda, Kakō, *Jūgun Ianfu* (Military Comfort Women), Futabasha, Tokyo, (1973).

4 Soh, p.38.

5 Bentley, Jerry H., and Ziegler, Herbert F., *Traditions and Encounters: A Global Perspective on the Past*, 4th Ed., McGraw-Hill Higher Education, New York, (2008), p.1053.

B. Conflation with *Teishintai/Chongsindae*

Whereas comfort stations have started appearing in the early 1930s, the need to deal with the increasing demand for comfort women across occupied territories did not take place until after the outbreak of the Second Sino-Japanese War in 1937 as Japan's war efforts continued to escalate from that point on.[1] Japan's military had less than a total of one million soldiers in 1937, but more men were mobilized each year, almost hitting the three million mark by 1943.[2]

After the bombing of Pearl Harbor on December 8, 1941, Korean and Taiwanese men joined the Imperial Japanese Forces.[3] The heightened military engagement at all levels resulted in the formation of the *Joshi Rōdō Teishintai* (hereinafter *teishintai*), the Women's Volunteer Labor Corps consisting of unmarried young girls and women between twelve and 39 years old. Through an August 1944 ordinance, the *teishintai* (*chongsindae* in Korean) labor force was mobilized to support Japan's aircraft manufacturing and other integral industries for the war effort, with the original term of one year that subsequently protracted for 24 months.[4]

For over two decades, the activists of the comfort women redress movement recited the number of victims at (or up to) 200,000 as can be seen in inscriptions of the statues

---

1 Nagasawa, p.8.

2 Yoshida, Yutaka, *Ajia Taiheiyō Sensō: Shiriizu Nihon Kindaishi 6* (Asia-Pacific War: Modern Japanese History Series, Volume 6), Iwanami Shoten, Publishers, Tokyo, (2007), p.95.

3 Soh, pp.38, 62.

4 Ibid., p.18.

and monuments in North America (refer to Prologue). The other chief claim of the narrative has been the majority of the women having been Korean. But what has become clear is the fact that most of them labored in China. Of the 400 comfort station locations, 280 were identified in China as of September of 1942.[5] It is not clear, however, if 400 was the number of locations where comfort stations were found or the actual numbers of comfort stations. Even according to the statistical analysis published by Korean Council and Ministry of Gender Equality in 2002, the majority of the Korean women were sent to China including Manchuria and Taiwan.[6]

The 200,000 figure first appeared in an article in 1970 by *Seoul Sinmun*, a national daily newspaper in South Korea.[7] Written by reporter Kim Tok-song, the piece stated that "From 1943 to 1945 approximately two hundred thousand Korean and Japanese women were mobilized as *chongsindae*. The estimated number of Koreans among them is between fifty and seventy thousand (emphasis added)."[8] Eleven years later, another Korean national newspaper *Hanguk Ilbo* featured Professor Yun Chong-ok's essay asserting that of the 200,000 **Korean women** in that same time period, between 50,000 and 70,000 had been "selectively sent as comfort women to the front lines in northern China and the Pacific Islands."[9] In the 1970 article by Kim Tok-song, the selected

---

5 Hata, p.400.

6 Soh, p.139.

7 Ibid., p.20.

8 Ibid.

9 Ibid., p.19.

tens of thousands of women are described as " 'playthings' of starved soldiers."[10]

Based on the statistical data sponsored by the South Korean Ministry of Gender Equality covering 190 cases of former comfort women, 76.8% had been recruited prior to 1943[11], a clear majority, rendering both newspaper articles somewhat far-fetched if not factually unfounded. In fact, the data "unequivocally reveals that the great majority of Korean survivors could not have been recruited as *chongsindae*."[12] On a more fundamental point, the two aforementioned newspaper articles unquestionably conflated comfort women with *chongsindae* as one entity or a subdivision of a larger group.

South Korea's foremost organization for the comfort women redress movement continues to be Korean Council for Women Drafted for Military Sexual Slavery by Japan (hereinafter ChongDaeHyup), founded back in November 1990. This activist organization's Korean name is *Chongsindae-munje Taechaek Hyopuihoe* which revealingly includes the term *chongsindae* that can be viewed as a powerful indication of how comfort women have been perceived by the Korean population for decades.

After researching over a hundred cases of former Korean comfort women, Professor Soh only found five to claim having been recruited as *chongsindae* and were later transported to China or Japan to serve as comfort women.[13] Yet, of the five cases, only two "appear to qualify as having been "real"

---

10 Ibid., p.20.

11 Ibid., p.62.

12 Ibid.

13 Ibid., p.58

chongsindae-turned-comfort women"[14] The circumstances do not corroborate any link, direct or otherwise, between the recruitment for *chongsindae* and being taken away to become comfort women. Instead, even though Soh maintains that since 1941, the term *chongsindae* in colonial Korea referred to different "patriotic" organizations of ordinary citizens to partake in supporting Japan's war effort, there is simply no documentary evidence "that proves the Chongsindae were used as comfort women."[15]

Furthermore, what Soh believes to be noticeably absent in the South Korean public discourse relates to the social class structure that existed during the wartime mobilization of women laborers including comfort women.[16] Contrary to almost all Korean comfort women who "came from the lower classes," two founding corepresentatives of ChongDaeHyup were "age mates" of the surviving comfort women that embodied the more privileged class that had access to education and other privileges.[17] The latter belonged to urban middle-class families of which some even went on to graduate schools and never had to worry about becoming *chongsindae* or comfort women.[18] Even so, with the very term being part of its official name, ChongDaeHyup engages in a "successful political strategy to represent comfort women as forcibly recruited *chongsindae*" (not *wianbu* which connotes prostitutes) that advances a patently disputable contention

---

14 Ibid.

15 Ibid., pp.58-59.

16 Ibid., p.59.

17 Ibid., p.60.

18 Ibid.

and a narrative "far from the factual truth disclosed in South Korean survivors' testimonials."[19]

The continuous use of *chongsindae* as part of its identity by ChongDaeHyup invites unnecessary confusion in at least two respects: a) the term specifically refers to the mobilized female volunteers from late 1943 and particularly from August 1944 to support the war efforts per the ordinance; and b) former Korean comfort women themselves were not familiar with the term until being told about it decades later.[20] Nevertheless, *chongsindae* serves as a "nationalist euphemism" as opposed to other terms with stereotypical negative impressions of sexual laborers, thereby protecting the dignity of the former comfort women.[21]

---

19 Ibid., p.74

20 Ibid., pp.18, 62.

21 Ibid., p.62.

C. First Comfort Station in Shanghai, China

Relying on existing documentary evidence, the first comfort station specifically set up for the Imperial Japanese army personnel opened in early April of 1932.[1] With the military designating a building as a comfort station and a proprietor employing women mainly from Southern Japan, the operational guidelines more or less mirrored those that U.S. soldiers noted in their military reports years later. Use of condoms and antiseptics by the soldiers, registering each comfort woman's information (name, birthplace, age, *résumé*, etc.) with the military police, a military doctor conducting physical exams of the women every week, and women to only receive military servicemen are enumerated as part of the rules and regulations.[2] This very first army-designated comfort station had to close its doors after two months when the troops pulled out of the area.[3] Thus, even if comfort stations appeared all over different territories, reasons for abrupt closures or relocations always existed given the ever-changing circumstances on the battlefield.

Another element that cannot be ignored relates to the 'military-run' comfort stations. Obviously lacking the business skills compared to seasoned proprietors, it has been argued that these facilities managed by the military served as a transient response to the sexual needs of the troops.[4] In other words, they were subsequently replaced by comfort

---

1 Hata, pp.64-65.

2 Ibid., p.64.

3 Ibid., p.65.

4 Ibid., pp.80-81.

stations professionally run by proprietors if determined viable from a business standpoint. Although statistics are not available to substantiate the claim, most of these comfort stations directly run by military personnel may have disappeared by 1938, but some survived as brothels catering to the smallest units of the Japanese military stationed in rural areas.[5]

---

5 Ibid.

D. Estimates Based on Military Records

The difficulty in arriving at a realistic, fairly accurate number of comfort women lies in the fact that they were not part of the Japanese military personnel even as civilian employees. Unlike the sexual laborers in Japan proper and other colonial territories such as Korea and Taiwan who were registered with the police, comfort women's registration took place at comfort stations in occupied territories while battles were being fought. While maintained at the local or larger regional level, there does not seem to be any indication of their records having been submitted to or collected by the military central command in Tokyo, Japan.[1]

Gordon Thomas, the Australian POW in Rabaul wrote in his diary that over 3,000 women (what he referred to as "Little Ladies") arrived to take care of some 100,000 men. The fact appears, however, that while he was correct about the approximate size of the troops, the U.S. Strategic Bombing Survey assessed the number of comfort women to be between 500 and 600.[2]

In determining a reasonably reliable estimate of the total number of comfort women, Professor Hata considered different methods such as relying on the ratio between comfort women and the soldiers, basing it on the number of comfort stations that existed, focusing on the bottom line

---

[1] Hata, p. 397

[2] The United States Strategic Bombing Survey (Pacific) The Allied Campaign against Rabaul, Naval Analysis Division, Washington, 1946, p.35.

of operating comfort stations, and examining the Japanese military's allotment of condoms to the troops.[3]

The earliest Japanese military document dealing with the issue of how many comfort women were needed for a particular territory utilized the ratio of one per 100 men.[4] Other ratios between the women and soldiers that were supposedly considered or approximated by those on the battlegrounds range from one per 40 to 600.[5]

As for making an estimate based on the number of comfort stations, if the total number had been 400 and with the average number of women between ten and twenty being the accepted range from actual case studies, that would make the number of women between 4,000 and 8,000. Utilizing a multiplier of 1.5 for peak periods when Japan mobilized the maximum number of soldiers, the range will then be between 6,000 and 12,000.[6]

A rather curious analysis from a financial standpoint concerns both the soldiers as customers and operating the comfort station as a viable business. The parameters are as follows: a) a typical soldier, at most, was able to visit a comfort station on average once a month given his income; b) for a comfort woman to repay the advanced loan in one to two years would have needed 2,000 customers a year, a monthly average of 150~160, and the proprietor would have required that much business transaction to keep her

---

[3] Hata, p.398.

[4] Ibid., p.403. A report by Dr. Matsumura, 21st Army Division, Military Medical Director, presented at the Head Chiefs Conference, Dept. of the Army, April 15, 1939 is cited.

[5] Ibid., p.406.

[6] Ibid., pp.400-402.

employed.[7] By applying such fundamentals of supply and demand, a researcher arrived at a ratio of one comfort woman per 150 soldiers, thereby calculating the total number of women between 20,000 and 30,000.[8]

But perhaps determining the approximate number of comfort women may be most effective based upon how many condoms had been supplied to the troops by the military. For the year of 1942, the Department of Army records show 32.1 million condoms as part of the supplies list for troops in the battlefield – this converts to 88,000 condoms a day (32,100,000 / 365 days ≈ 88,000), and the challenge lies in how many soldiers a typical comfort woman dealt with each day.[9] Professor Hata proffers his estimation by setting the total number of soldiers at three million on all battlefronts, and 88,000 a day would essentially reflect each soldier going to a comfort station once every 30 days.[10]

By factoring the daily average of five customers for a sexual laborer in Japan proper, the necessary number of comfort women would be 17,600 (17,600 x 5 = 88,000) and having ten a day would reduce it to 8,800. Conversely, by raising the number of comfort women to 176,000 that gets very close to the 200,000 claim, three million soldiers would have needed to visit a comfort station every three days based upon an average of five customers a day.[11] Such frequent visits could not have been possible for many reasons including the soldiers' limited income and physical energy

---

7 Ibid., p.402.

8 Ibid.

9 Ibid.

10 Ibid.

11 Ibid.

Inconvenient and Uncomfortable 149

in the time of an ongoing war. This reality would still hold true even if the turnover rate among comfort women had been high. In fact, the prevailing narrative includes the number of soldiers comfort women had to service between 20 and 30 a day, sometimes even higher, which practically renders the high turnover issue irrelevant: 200,000 comfort women x 20~30 soldiers = four to six million a day. Either an enormous reduction in the number of women or their daily average must be worked out first.

In addition to the military records in condom allotment, the actual number of its consumption in the Shanghai area has also been discovered: 43,000 condoms by 140 comfort women in a month, which can be broken down to ten a day by each woman in a 30-day period.[12] This statistic recorded in 1942 includes a comment that condoms were given to soldiers every other month, and that an increase in supply was unnecessary.[13]

As for the number of Japanese soldiers who visited comfort stations, Hata feels three million to be unrealistically high in view of Japan's continuous setbacks since 1942 in the Pacific, and after more troops being mobilized from Japan proper and colonial territories, they had to engage in decisive battles soon after deployment.[14] The circumstances surrounding Japan in the war were rapidly changing for the worse, and going to comfort stations even once a month may not have been possible to many on the battlefront.

---

12 Ibid., p.404.

13 Ibid.

14 Ibid. In 1943, 2.2 million (out of 2.9) were stationed overseas, and the number increased to 2.87 million out of 4.1 in the following year. Yoshida, p.95.

Utilizing three million or slightly less for the number of Japanese troops outside of Japan can only be justified during its peak years, which would be during World War II. With Imperial Japan's military being significantly smaller in the 1930s (less than 300,000 between 1931 and 1936; almost one million soldiers in 1937), an average number must be considered for the entire fifteen years of the Pacific War. To complicate the matter further, for the comfort stations to survive, there must have been enough soldiers to seek sexual services on a continuous basis in a particular area. Therefore, it can be argued that a fair number of comfort stations may not have lasted long given the changing environment of the regional battles, making the task of arriving at an objective estimate evermore challenging.

Be that as it may, a rational bases for a calculation can be as follows:

a) 270,000 as the average size of the troops between 1931 and 1936, with 75% stationed overseas (270,000 x 75% = 202,500); 917,500 between 1937 and 1940[15]; 2,500,000 during World War II per Professor Hata's estimation[16];

b) one comfort woman per 100~150 soldiers.

202,500 x 6 years + 917,500 x 4 years + 2,500,000 x 5 years / 15 years = 1,159,000 as the average in 15 years;

---

15 Morimoto, Tadao, *Makuro Keizaigaku kara mita Taiheiyō Sensō* (The Pacific War from a Macroeconomic Viewpoint), PHP Shinsho, Tokyo, (2005), pp.329-330. 720,000 stationed overseas in 1937, 920,000 in 1938, 1 million in 1939, and 1.03 million in 1940. Reasonable percentage of overseas troops set at 75% for previous years.

16 Hata, p.404.

1,159,000 soldiers / 100~150 = 7,726 ~ 11,590 comfort women

With a turnover rate of 1.5 in China and Manchuria[17] where comfort stations appeared earliest and the territories being the main areas for comfort stations (280 out of 400 or 70%) factored in, the total would range between 10,430 (7,726 x 70% x 1.5 + 7,726 x 30% x 1) and 15,646 (11,590 x 70% x 1.5 + 11,590 x 30% x 1). This range does not deviate from results of other methods previously explored; in fact it reinforces many of them, and figures that double or even triple it must have sound reasoning backed by empirical, numerical facts.

While no roster or other registration materials for a large number of comfort women have been unearthed, quantitative data on Japan's military machine are sufficiently available. In other words, the 'demand' for comfort women can be reasonably determined, and at this point to further challenge the 200,000 narrative is unnecessary - its sheer number cannot be justified when other allegations such as the many men they serviced daily takes it to an even more surreal, implausible realm of conjecture.

---

17 Ibid., p.406. This turnover rate has been utilized by other scholars.

Conclusion

Even scholars who have done substantial research on the issue of comfort women have faced difficulty in addressing the numbers question. Several have offered ranges such as between 50,000 and 200,000 (Yoshimi), treating the figure 200,000 as somehow factually established. Nothing can be further from the truth as its source indubitably dealt with *teishintai/chongsindae*, and the conflation with comfort women continues to this day through a legion of activists headed by the likes of ChongDaeHyup.

If a more serious study involving the size of Japan's military and other elements crucial to operate comfort stations is undertaken, rather than hysterically reciting the grossly exaggerated numbers of the women and their daily output, the numbers question would be just another uninteresting exercise in basic arithmetic supported by common sense. The total number of women and their daily average of customers must maintain an inverse proportion because the size of Japan's military during the Pacific War has not changed since its conclusion over 70 years ago. Yet, the propagandists advancing the prevailing narrative has inflated the number of women to 400,000 in recent years, and a 2015 Broadway musical on comfort women described the women's ordeal as having to deal with up to 100 men a day.

Whereas activists of the comfort women redress movement appear via media outlets whenever possible, the largest group of former Korean comfort women remain an "invisible and silent cluster."[18] As a scholar who has met many of the women, Professor Soh proclaims that this "great majority have completely stayed out of the limelight."[19] At least one former comfort woman concluded that some are "imposters" who spread lies about the living conditions in the comfort stations.[20]

But perhaps a more fundamental inquiry becomes necessary since the numbers question has not been particularly settled objectively. While scholars in favor of the redress movement who have taken the time to do research tend to offer very broad ranges of the number of women involved (i.e., 50,000 to 200,000), baseless allegations such as "many were killed by the retreating Japanese troops"[21] continue to be part of the movement's rhetoric. Needless to say, without even substantiating a reasonably objective figure of the subject matter involved, it makes absolutely no sense accusing the Japanese military to have exterminated a large portion of the women.

---

18 Soh, p.93.

19 Ibid.

20 Ibid., p.97.

21 U.N. ESCOR, 52D Sess., U.N. Doc. E/CN.4 (1196), p.7. Testimonial narratives by former comfort women do not include massacres but how they returned to their homeland. It is fair to say that the vast majority of the women returned to Korea while others remained in parts of Asia for various reasons. Park, p.128. It has been argued that proprietors who had recruited them were responsible for their safe return, but the women were often abandoned after Japan's surrender. Ibid., p.120.

PART IV

Putting Things in Perspective
for the 21st Century

A. Other Military Brothels Since World War II

Although the world had rejoiced in the Allied Forces' eventual decisive victory over the Axis Powers and hoped for a peaceful second half of the 20th century, vicious regional wars continued to break out in the Pacific, transforming it into one of the main arenas for a geopolitical, hegemonic battleground. The United States military participated in both the Korean War and Vietnam War to confront the threat of Communism spreading in parts of Asia, with China emerging as a major military power under the leadership of Chairman Mao.

As a consequence of any military deployment, the sexual needs of the soldiers lingered as an inherent part of military affairs, albeit not a matter brought to the fore, and brothels catering to the military with some degree of government involvement came into being in both South Korea and Vietnam. In South Korea, numerous camptowns such as American Town approximate to or adjoined to major U.S. military camps served as a place for 'rest and relaxation' for the troops.[1] Park Chung-hee, South Korea's president from 1963 until his assassination in 1979, encouraged women to earn U.S. dollars for the country, and his signed document "Camptown Clean-up Measures" dated May 2, 1977 dealt with a network of brothels that serviced the U.S. military.[2]

---

1 Moon, Kathleen, *Sex Among Allies*, Columbia University Press, New York, (1977), p.17.

2 Lee, J-k. (Nov. 6, 2013) Management of camptown women – document signed by South Korean President Park Chung-hee disclosed. Hankyoreh. (http://www.hani.co.kr/arti/society/women/610074.html)

Unfortunately, the exploitation of the female laborers by the proprietors and managers of the brothels proved not uncommon, such as not paying the percentage of their services that would lead to borrowing money for various reasons (for medical treatment and to send funds to their families), further forcing them into debt.[3] Women sold drinks and their bodies and the club owners took around 80% of the share.[4]

In June 2014, 123 Korean comfort women filed a lawsuit against the South Korean government to reclaim "human dignity and proper compensation."[5]

The women accused the government of encouraging them to serve as "patriots" and "civilian diplomats" as it "trained them and worked with pimps to run a sex trade" for the U.S. military stationed in South Korea in the 1960s and 1970s."[6]

In what would be regarded as a landmark ruling, on January 17, 2017, a three-judge panel of the Central District Court in Seoul held that the South Korean government had illegally detained prostitutes to undergo forced treatment for sexually transmitted diseases, ordering payment of about US$4,240 to each of the 57 women to compensate for physical

---

3 Moon, p.21.

4 Ibid., p.131. Mistreatment of the women included physical assault and psychological harassment. Ibid., pp.90-91.

5 Park, J-m. (July 11, 2014) Former Korean 'comfort women' for U.S. troops sue own government. Reuters. (https://www.reuters.com/article/us-southkorea-usa-military/former-korean-comfort-women-for-u-s-troops-sue-own-government-idUSKBN0FG0VV20140711)

6 Ibid.

and psychological damage.[7] By drawing a comparison with Japan's comfort women system, the plaintiffs asserted that it was hypocritical of "South Korea to condemn Japan for its historical wrongdoings while not acknowledging its own role" in helping foreign soldiers have access to prostitutes.[8]

While the government neither offered an apology nor admit involvement in the creation and management of the brothel network in camptowns, the verdict acknowledged a "serious human rights violation" on the part of South Korea, making it the first time ever in admitting to having engaged in the illegal treatment of women.[9] In February 2018, the Seoul High Court ruled that the South Korean government "operated and managed" the military camptowns in order to, among other things, "boost morale among foreign troops."[10]

During the Vietnam War, military brothels on army base camps, the 'Sin Cities,' 'Disneylands,' or 'boom-boom parlors' for the American soldiers were set up to deal with their sexual urges.[11] Vietnam (formerly the easternmost part of Indochina) has had a tradition of brothels for foreign

---

7   Choe, S-h. (Jan. 20, 2017) South Korea Illegally Held Prostitutes Who Catered to G.I.s Decades Ago, Court Says. New York Times-Asia Pacific. (https://www.nytimes.com/2017/01/20/world/asia/south-korea-court-comfort-women.html) The court concluded that the rest of the women did not sufficiently prove their case of being victims of the government's illegal acts.

8   Ibid.

9   Ibid.

10 Eigenramm, A. (March 3, 2018) Korea's 'patriotic prostitutes' for US soldiers get justice at last. Asia Times. (http://www.atimes.com/article/koreas-patriotic-prostitutes-us-soldiers-get-justice-last/)

11 Brownmiller, Susan, *Against Her Will*, Ballantine Books, New York, (1975), p.95.

troops that long predated the American presence as the French Army's *Bordel Militaire de Campagne*, the mobile field brothel, comprised of women from Algeria, traveled with the troops in the combat zones.[12]

After the Americans replaced the French, the war escalated and so did the demand for sexual laborers.[13] A representation of a 'recreation area' for the U.S. soldiers was the Lai Khe which belonged to the base camp of the 3rd Brigade, 1st Infantry Division. Located 25 miles north of Saigon, this one-acre compound was surrounded by barbed wire and American MPs standing guard at the gate.[14] The main attraction inside the compound was two concrete barracks, each roughly one hundred feet long – they were military brothels that serviced the soldiers.[15]

The U.S. military controlled and regulated the health and security features of the brothels, and the women's share was 40%, with an average of eight to ten customers a day. It has been said that the Lai Khe women made more than the U.S. soldiers.[16]

In another base located in Long Binh, a militarized city of 25,000 people, sexual laborers were officially welcomed there as "local national guests."[17] The base employed hundreds of Vietnamese women as service personnel and were referred

---

12 Ibid., p.93.

13 Ibid., pp.93-94.

14 Ibid., p.94.

15 Ibid., p.95.

16 Ibid.

17 Enloe, Cynthia, *Does Khaki Become You?*, South End Press, Boston, (1983), p.33.

to by military men as "mama-sans"[18] and "hooch-girls." Soldiers also brought other women just off base as "local national guests."[19]

But a comment below may be a disturbing reality as to how some soldiers felt about paying for sexual services:

> Let's face it. Nature is nature. There are women available. Those women are of another culture, another colour, another society. You don't want a prostitute. You've got an M-16. What do you need to pay for a lady for? You go down to the village and you take what you want.[20]

Although utterly revolting, this revealing sentiment cannot be deemed a complete aberration as Japan's comfort women system apparently did not prevent rape and violence by certain members of its military in occupied enemy territories.

---

18 Mama-san often refers to the female manager or proprietor of a brothel in certain Asian cultures.

19 Enloe, p.33.

20 Ibid., pp.33-34.

B. Japan's Past Compensations, Reparations, and Apologies

On June 22, 1965, after almost a fifteen-year-long negotiation process, Japan and South Korea agreed to normalize diplomatic relations in the spirit of the United Nations by signing the Treaty on Basic Relations between Japan and the Republic of Korea.[1] In a separate document entitled Agreement on the Settlement of Problems Concerning Property and Claims and on Economic Co-operation between Japan and the Republic of Korea, Japan agreed to proceed with a US$800 million financial package for South Korea in grants and loans to resolve the "problem concerning property, rights and interests of the two Contracting Parties and their nationals (including juridical persons)" and that the claims between the two nations and their people have been "settled completely and finally."[2]

Since the advent of the comfort women redress movement, activists have contended that the negotiation talks of this 1965 Treaty and Agreement did not address the issue of comfort women or that individual claims by the comfort women against Japan are valid regardless of them.[3] In January 2005,

---

[1] Treaty on Basic Relations between Japan and the Republic of Korea, June 22, 1965. (http://worldjpn.grips.ac.jp/documents/texts/docs/19650622.T1E.html)

[2] Agreement on the Settlement of Problems Concerning Property and Claims and on Economic Co-operation between Japan and the Republic of Korea, Article II, Item 1, June 22, 1965. (http://worldjpn.grips.ac.jp/documents/texts/JPKR/19650622.T9E.html)

[3] Japan had requested payments to individuals for the 1965 financial arrangement, but they were received by South Korea as a nation. Park, pp.186-187.

South Korea declassified documents that purport to preclude any "further compensation demands, either at the government level or individual level" as a result of the consummation of the 1965 economic cooperation arrangement.[4]

During the negotiation process with Japan, South Korea's intentions were to "assume the responsibility for compensating individuals after resolving all claims including individual ones on a lump sum basis. Propriety by item, criteria and methods for individual compensation will be worked out."[5]

It has become the general understanding today that once receiving the funds from Japan, the government engaged in aggressive "large-scale economic projects" by sacrificing compensation for individuals. The government has maintained its stance that not only is legal compensation for individuals "difficult to implement," it "has no legal responsibility to compensate" them.[6] More documents on the 1965 negotiations have been declassified since.[7]

On August 4, 1993, as the comfort women issue was gathering momentum as a human rights matter at the international level, Japan's Chief Cabinet Secretary Yōhei Kōno extended the nation's "sincere apologies and remorse to all those, irrespective of place of origin, who suffered

---

[4] S.Korea Discloses Sensitive Documents. (Jan. 17, 2005). UPI. (https://www.upi.com/SKorea-discloses-sensitive-documents/38131105952315/?spt=su)

[5] Compensation for Colonial Victims Is Not Just a Legal Problem. (Jan. 17, 2005). Chosun Ilbo. (http://english.chosun.com/site/data/html_dir/2005/01/17/2005011761043.html)

[6] Ibid.

[7] Declassified Documents Could Trigger Avalanche of Lawsuits. (May 31, 2015). Chosun Ilbo. (http://english.chosun.com/site/data/html_dir/2005/01/17/2005011761025.html)

immeasurable pain and incurable physical and psychological wounds as comfort women."[8]

Although this was not the first public apology made by a member of Japan's government concerning the comfort women issue[9], it was the most widely broadcast by the media at that time, and these words of apology have been subsequently referred to as the Kōno Statement. While Japan acknowledged then military involvement in the establishment, management, and transport of the women, it makes certain points quite clear, in particular regarding the recruiting process:

> The recruitment of the comfort women was conducted mainly by private recruiters who acted in response to the request of the military. The Government study has revealed that in many cases they were recruited against their own will, through coaxing, coercion, etc., and that, at times, administrative/military personnel directly took part in the recruitments.[10]

The Kōno Statement has been viewed as an admission of 'indirect coercion' by Japan as a sovereign nation, for such type of recruitment transpired within Japanese territories.[11] The military's direct involvement in the recruiting is qualified by "at times," and this point has been rather sufficiently substantiated through previous sections in this study.

---

8 Statement by the Chief Cabinet Secretary Yōhei Kōno on the result of the study on the issue of "comfort women", August 4, 1993, (hereinafter "Kōno Statement") (http://www.mofa.go.jp/policy/women/fund/state9308.html).

9 Prime Minister Kiichi Miyazawa made a series of apologies in January 1992.

10 Kōno Statement.

11 Park, pp.235-237.

A few years later, Japan addressed the issue of comfort women in a comprehensive, proactive manner, reaching out to the survivors of different nationalities by establishing the Asian Women's Fund (hereinafter AWF) on June 14, 1995. Spearheaded by then Prime Minister Murayama, the ethos of this Fund was to express the Japanese government's "awareness, remorse and apologies concerning the comfort women issue as expressed in the 1993 statement by Chief Cabinet Secretary Yohei Kono."[12]

Over a term of twelve years, the AWF provided atonement money (2 million yen each) to 285 former comfort women, a medical welfare support system in the countries where the women resided, not to mention collecting and editing historical documents on the issue to "reflect on past mistakes of violating women's dignity and assist projects that deal with current women's issues such as violence."[13] In addition to the atonement money, a letter of apology from the prime minister was delivered to each comfort woman.[14]

Approximately 5.4 billion yen (about US$50 million, with 90 percent being public funds) was collected by the AWF to compensate the women in Indonesia, the Netherlands, the Philippines, South Korea, and Taiwan through various means.[15] By the time the AWF was officially dissolved, 364

---

12 The Statement by President of the Asian Women's Fund at the Final Press Conference, March 6, 2007. (http://www.awf.or.jp/e3/dissolution.html). An official statement by Prime Minister Murayama regarding the AWF: http://www.awf.or.jp/e6/statement-08-2.html

13 Ibid.

14 Ibid. Copy of a letter by the prime minister: http://www.awf.or.jp/e6/statement-12.

15 History Issues Q & A: Q5, Overview of the activities of the Asian Women's Fund. Ministry of Foreign Affairs of Japan. (http://www.mofa.go.jp/policy/q_a/faq16.html)

comfort women survivors received some form of financial compensation.[16]

With ChongDaeHyup, the perennial driving force of the redress movement, taking "adamant opposition" to the AWF[17], the majority of the former comfort women in South Korea refused to accept any atonement money.[18] ChongDaeHyup maintains its position to pressure Japan to take legal responsibility for implementing the comfort women system and the suffering it has caused, with Japan committing to public compensation as the desired solution.[19]

---

16 Soh, p.239.

17 Ibid., p.96. The South Korean government arranged certain funds to the women on condition that they would not receive anything from Japan. Park, p.190.

18 As of 2002, 61 out of 135 Korean women (45%) then living accepted the atonement money from Japan. (https://www.mofa.go.jp/policy/women/fund/policy.html)

19 Park, p.172.

C. The 2015 Accord with South Korea

On December 28, 2015, in the final month of a year that marked the 70-year anniversary of the conclusion of World War II, Japan and South Korea held a joint announcement by their foreign ministers as follows:

> 1.(1)(i); The issue of comfort women, with an involvement of the Japanese military authorities at that time, was a grave affront to the honor and dignity of large numbers of women, and the Government of Japan is painfully aware of responsibilities from this perspective. As Prime Minister of Japan, Prime Minister Abe expresses anew his most sincere apologies and remorse to all the women who underwent immeasurable and painful experiences and suffered incurable physical and psychological wounds as comfort women.
>
> 1.(2)(i); The Government of the ROK [Republic of Korea] values the GOJ's announcement and efforts made by the Government of Japan in the lead-up to the issuance of the announcement and confirms, together with the GOJ, that the issue is resolved finally and irreversibly with this announcement, on the premise that the Government of Japan will steadily implement the measures specified in 1.(1)(ii) above. The Government of the ROK will cooperate

in the implementation of the Government of Japan's measures.[1]

Per the Accord, Japan agreed to a one-time contribution to provide "support for the former comfort women" through a foundation established by the South Korean government.[2] Additionally, South Korea agreed to "refrain from accusing or criticizing each other regarding this issue in the international community, including at the United Nations, on the premise that the Government of Japan will steadily implement the measures it announced."[3] The following year, Japan kept its part of the Accord by remitting 1 billion yen (US$8.8 million) to South Korea, and 34 out of the 46 comfort women survivors either received compensation or expressed their intention to accept it.[4]

The opposition to the Accord, the activists and other former comfort women, voiced a number of problems, from the women not being a part of the negotiation, insincerity on Japan's part for not meeting the women, the Accord not being "legally binding," to the amount of compensation being inadequate. A lawsuit was filed by twelve women against the Accord in September 2016, and an independent task force commissioned by South Korea's Foreign Ministry noted "problems in the pre-deal process" in its 31-page report.[5]

---

1 Announcement by Foreign Ministers of Japan and the Republic of Korea at the Joint Press Occasion, Dec. 28, 2015. (http://www.mofa.go.jp/a_o/na/kr/page4e_000365.html)

2 Ibid., 1(1)(ii).

3 Ibid., 1(2)(iii).

4 Salmon, A. (Dec. 27, 2017) Probe Casts Shadow Over 'Comfort Women' Deal. Asia Times. (http://www.atimes.com/article/probe-casts-shadow-comfort-women-deal/)

5 Ibid.

The impeachment of Park Geun-hye, the president of South Korea at the time the deal had been struck, did not help either, and a majority of the Korean population continues to be against the Accord that garnered strong support from Washington.[6]

The removal of the comfort woman statue in front of the Japanese embassy in Seoul, or taking sincere steps to "strive to solve this issue in an appropriate manner"[7], a commitment South Korea agreed to in the Accord, is all but forgotten as a new statue appeared facing the Japanese Consulate in Pusan (or Busan), the second largest city in South Korea. It is fair to say that the activists (and some women survivors) will continue to demand a more 'sincere apology' and formal reparations by Japan founded on the acceptance of legal responsibility of the injuries caused by the comfort women system.

---

6 According to Realmeter, a South Korean polling firm, 63.2% was for rescinding the Accord and another 20.5% felt not rescinding and renegotiating with Japan was a mistake. Mun Je-in Seiken no Shijisō wa Kangei, Nihon no 'Hōteki Sekinin' mo; Hoshukei wa Tainichi Kankei Akka Kenen (Supporters of Moon's Administration Welcomes New Policy as well as Japan's 'Legal Responsibility' Theory: Conservatives Express Concerns of Deteriorating Relations with Japan). (Jan. 11, 2017). Sankei News. (https://www.sankei.com/world/news/180111/wor1801110032-n1.html)

7 Announcement by Foreign Ministers of Japan and the Republic of Korea at the Joint Press Occasion, Dec. 28, 2015, 1.(2)(ii).

D. Transcending the Comfort Women Paradigm

In Part I, II, and III, three specific elements comprising the prevailing narrative (i.e., the paradigmatic story), the a) institutionalized, systematic abduction, forcible recruitment or conscription; b) of up to or more than 200,000 women; c) for sexual slavery by Imperial Japan, were explored and analyzed through a multitude of materials including original source documents such as the U.S. military reports during World War II.

The materials presented in this study offered enlightening information and invaluable perspectives in making a more comprehensive, balanced evaluation of Japan's military brothel system. The notion of a state-sponsored sexual slavery system involving a systematically-organized illegal and immoral military operation has never been part of any statements of apology by the Japanese government all these years. Instead, what has been reiterated are words of "sincere apologies and remorse" extended to all the women who suffered "incurable physical and psychological wounds."

These words of apology and remorse, insofar as what this study has shown along with the findings by governments of Japan and South Korea[1], should be taken as an acceptance of responsibility for all the injuries and sufferings caused by the nation of Japan for implementing a military brothel system, <u>not an admission of having engaged in an institutionalized, systematic criminal act of seizing defenseless women by the Imperial Forces for the purpose of sexual enslavement</u>.

---

1 Such as the joint investigation report issued in July 1992.

Professor Park of South Korea has contended that the actual perpetrators of deceptive recruiting and other illegal methods to procure women, namely the recruiters and proprietors, should be held accountable in addition to the nation of Japan.[2] Going a step further, if Japan is to be held 'legally responsible' for the injuries caused by the comfort women system, strict examination of the specific facts including the illegal and immoral acts by these perpetrators must be undertaken. For any government to take legal responsibility, an appropriate legal procedure is called for and clear evidence must be produced as opposed to testimonial narratives.[3] But with so many former comfort women already gone and others advanced in age, such undertaking at this time is both impracticable and unreasonable. Instead, by Japan taking responsibility by way of a series of apologies and monetary settlements, credit must be given where credit is due.

* * *

Before the turn of the nineteenth century, the term *karayuki-san*, originally referring to the young women of Japan that emigrated to China or other parts of Asia to seek work, gradually came to denote the daughters of tender age from impoverished families who were "sold into overseas prostitution."[4] These young girls settled in licensed quarters in Korea, parts of China, then across South East Asia, and aside from the single men who migrated for better opportunities, they also serviced soldiers on the battlefield

---

2 Park, p.34.

3 Hata, p.177.

4 Soh, p.114.

as Japan expanded its military footprint.[5] These sexual laborers were indeed precursors of Japan's comfort women during the Pacific War, many of whom already residing on the Korean Peninsula before its annexation by Japan in 1910.[6]

In subsequent years, these women were given another term *rōshigun* (or *jōshigun* which literally means women's army), i.e., although struggling in the type of work for the lowest social order, they were referred to as soldiers as they willingly responded to the calls of the military (representing their motherland) as patriots.[7] The *rōshigun*, or more collectively *karayuki-san*, served to satiate the hometown nostalgia that included sexual comfort, easing the men's minds toward their motherland[8], whether they were fighting in a war or not as in either case the men were engaging in a form of economic expansion overseas.

The term comfort woman in Japanese, '*ianfu*,' is comprised of '*ian* – 慰安' which means 'to comfort the heart of the person for his efforts' and '*fu* - 婦' for 'woman.' In essence, a comfort woman refers to a woman who comforts the man (the soldier) for his military service, and though the sexual aspects cannot be ignored, her company, even for a very brief moment in an intensely violent, dangerous environment unquestionably provided a sense of psychological, spiritual repose. While the activists and their allies have called comfort women as some euphemism for brutalized sex slaves, the use of the term '*ianfu*' by Imperial Japan must have reflected its belief

---

5 Park, pp.34-36.

6 Ibid., p.37.

7 Ibid., p.38.

8 Ibid., p.35, 39.

in regarding the women as much more than sexual laborers.[9] Additional functions as nurses have been documented and mentioned by former comfort women including Mun Ok-chu.[10] Civilians from Japan proper, often children, shipped 'comfort bags' to the soldiers containing groceries, medicine, loincloths, and letters of encouragement.[11] When the bags were received by the troops, the items were also distributed to the comfort women, especially lipstick and wooden clogs.[12]

There is an important point that must be reminded once again. The comfort women system was developed, among other reasons, to prevent troops from committing violent acts against the local populace, in particular the women. Unfortunately, this study has shown that certain members of the Japanese military nevertheless engaged in violence such as rape, but the comfort stations were not, conceptually and through implementation, meant as locales for such acts. If harming others through violence had been the objective, paying a fee and also dealing with strict rules and regulations enforced at the comfort stations would have been more than irrational. The soldiers only had two choices, and going to a comfort station was what their military superiors expected them to do.

More than six decades have passed since the demilitarized zone was designated on the Korean Peninsula, and as the U.S. military maintains its presence in South Korea, non-Korean sexual laborers from Russia and China have been

---

9 If not, having a term such as 'comfort woman' was probably unnecessary.

10 Soh, p.125.

11 Ibid., p.136.

12 Ibid., pp.136-137.

replacing those from the Philippines and Peru.[13] As long as wars are being fought, and as long as some anticipation of a war persists, there will be a demand for sexual laborers, and the most vulnerable women from destitute backgrounds will 'sell' their only resource – their bodies.[14] In this respect, a glaring parallel between men who enlist in the military as their only option for employment and these women can be easily drawn. Whereas the women offer their bodies as collateral, the soldiers sign away their lives[15], so in a sense, they are 'brothers and sisters' for the military effort.

The comfort women issue, if viewed as the military's response to the physical as well as, to some extent, the psychological needs of the troops, notwithstanding the disparity in the degree of its involvement in the management, supervision, and even the recruitment of the women – if some form of a military brothel system must be furnished for the sake of the troops (and safety of the local populace), it will be an ongoing controversial matter as long as there are military bases all over the world.

An argument can be made that Japan's comfort women system was a byproduct of its expansionist policy that necessitated the mobilization of men and some women. This aggressive expansionist policy led to the Russo-Japanese War, the annexation of Korea, and ultimately the Pacific War, but quite arguably, they were Japan's answer to Western colonialism all across Asia. Erecting comfort women statues and monuments in the United States symbolically (and perhaps practically) delegates America as the arbiter of the

---

13 Park, pp.293-294.

14 Ibid., pp.294-295.

15 Ibid., p.295.

very issue, but it also heightens the irony that U.S. forces remain stationed in both Japan and South Korea where sexual laborers continue to exist.[16]

The inscriptions of these statues and monuments such as "forcibly taken from their homes" and "abducted for the use of sexual slavery" fail to present the comfort women story as a whole (in particular the Japanese women); instead, it advances only the carefully crafted collective memory by the activists of the redress movement, what has been identified as the paradigmatic story. As a natural reaction to this activism, the other side has continued to rebut the paradigm with another collective memory – that the women were merely prostitutes.[17]

The paradigmatic story of women being forcibly taken away as sex slaves exposes a certain prejudice and stigmatization towards prostitution in society[18], and the counterargument that they were merely prostitutes incites even more turbulence to this emotional issue. Because of this unfortunate, unceasing dissension, the women's valuable function to the soldiers who sought physical and psychological comfort has been entirely forgotten.

Over 70 years have passed since the end of World War II, and it will be almost three decades since the comfort women issue became a subject of international controversy. Arguments for and against the paradigm have been made for years, and as we strive to make the 21st century a more peaceful and prosperous one, it is time to move forward with a new and different outlook for the future. It is time

---

16 Ibid., pp.171-172.

17 Ibid., p.158.

18 Ibid., p.320.

to recognize and fully accept the unpleasant realities of war and eulogize the women for the service only they were able to perform. It is time to transcend the comfort women paradigm, and this study will conclude with these words from a former comfort woman, Pae Chok-kan:

> Then, we were also soldiers. We were not prostitutes. We helped the soldiers to fight. Do you understand?[19]

---

19 Soh, p.189. Her words as she reflected on her days as a comfort woman.

Made in the USA
San Bernardino,
CA